Transmedia Archaeology

DOI: 10.1057/9781137434371.0001

Other Palgrave Pivot titles

Transmedia Archaeology: Storytelling in the Borderlines of Science Fiction, Comics and Pulp Magazines

Carlos A. Scolari
Universitat Pompeu Fabra, Spain

Paolo Bertetti
Università degli Studi di Siena, Italy

and

Matthew Freeman
Birmingham City University, UK

DOI: 10.1057/9781137434371.0001

First published 2014 by
PALGRAVE MACMILLAN

Palgrave Macmillan in the UK is an imprint of Macmillan Publishers Limited, registered in England, company number 785998, of Houndsmill, Basingstoke, Hampshire, RG21 6XS

Palgrave Macmillan in the US is a division of St Martin's Press LLC, 175 Fifth Avenue, New York, NY 10010.

Palgrave Macmillan is the global academic imprint of the above companies and has companies and representatives throughout the world.

Palgrave® and Macmillan® are registered trademarks in the United States, the United Kingdom, Europe and other countries

ISBN: 978-1-137-43438-8 EPUB
ISBN: 978-1-137-43437-1 PDF
ISBN: 978-1-137-43436-4 Hardback

This book is printed on paper suitable for recycling and made from fully managed and sustained forest sources. Logging, pulping and manufacturing processes are expected to conform to the environmental regulations of the country of origin.

A catalogue record for this book is available from the British Library.

A catalog record for this book is available from the Library of Congress.

www.palgrave.com/pivot

DOI: 10.1057/9781137434371

Contents

Foreword

I am pleased to write the foreword for a book that promises to make an important contribution to scholarly understandings of transmedia storytelling. Since Henry Jenkins first coined the term in 2003, both industry and academia have taken it up in their practice and analysis of practice respectively. Practitioners need not concern themselves with theoretical niceties; their success is measured by the production of popular and profitable content. But academic research succeeds to the degree that it produces a deep and nuanced understanding of the phenomena under study. Despite the ever increasing interest in and research on transmedia storytelling that this volume's bibliography attests to, researchers have to date focused primarily on the present and on the United States and occasionally on the United Kingdom. This volume's authors explicitly argue for the broadening of that focus to the past and to the rest of the world and implicitly argue for the employment of nuanced narratological theory in the analysis of transmedia storyworlds.

The authors' chief contribution is a call to historicise coupled with demonstrations of how to do it. To this end, they provide three compelling examples of the archaeology of transmedia – that is, of the transmedia construction of storyworlds that precede Jenkins' 2003 identification and labelling of a practice assumed to date from the late twentieth century. Some researchers have pointed to instances of the dispersion of narrative across different media forms in the past. However, few have so far provided detailed

DOI: 10.1057/9781137434371.0002

analyses of historical instances of a storytelling form that is usually seen as closely linked to twenty-first century media, industrial and technological convergence. As the authors assert, it is vital that we trace 'the relations between older storytelling practices and seemingly newer strategies of transmedia'. The book presents three case studies of science fiction/fantasy storyworlds first constructed in pulp novels or comics, demonstrating the significance of 'transmedia pulp fiction' as precursors and perhaps progenitors of today's vast transmedia narrative universes.

As George Santayana famously said, 'Those who cannot remember the past are condemned to repeat it.' Today's media practitioners may be unwittingly repeating their predecessors' practices, but they can function perfectly well in this state of ignorance. Academics, however, cannot. Reformulating Santayana, I would say that those who cannot remember the past are condemned to misunderstand the present. Conceiving of transmedia storytelling as arising solely from present conditions of media, industrial and technological convergence risks misunderstanding the phenomenon as being fully dependent on those conditions, rather than pre-existing them. Historicising the phenomenon as the authors do in the following pages reveals the contingency of present configurations and the storyworlds that they engender. In other words, transmedia storytelling depends upon alignments of media, industry and technologies that together spread a storyworld across multiple media platforms. But as this volume's case studies illustrate those alignments have varied significantly from those of today. The authors' analyses of divergent and quite specific historical conditions of production and reception reveals that today's transmedia storytelling is conditional upon the specificities of contemporary convergence. Past builders of transmedia storyworlds did things differently; future builders of such worlds will of necessity do things differently in response to inevitable shifts in underlying media, industrial and technological alignments. Just as media specificity, for example, the distinctions between film and television, is historically determined and not inherent so is transmedia storytelling not inherently tied to the present. Narrative universes emerged in the past and will emerge in the future but the means of building them differed and will differ from those employed today.

This volume also demonstrates that transmedia storytelling is not inherently tied to the United States or the other Anglophone countries in which some researchers, most notably Elizabeth Evans in the context of the United Kingdom, have explored the dispersion of content across

DOI: 10.1057/9781137434371.0002

media. Even among these countries, sharing as they do a common language and a common cultural heritage, storytelling practices vary according to different conditions of production and reception. For example, in a recent essay, I argue that two quite distinct contemporary Sherlock Holmes adaptations, the UK's *Sherlock* (BBC, 2010 to present) and the US' *Elementary* (CBS, 2011 to present), arose from the distinctions between the two countries' television industries.[1] Just as individual texts vary in accordance with their geographical conditions of production and reception, so do transmedia texts. Moving beyond the Anglophone world and into the territory of dictatorships and regime change, as does Carlos Scolari in his case study of Argentina's *El Eternauta*, shows not only that transmedia storytelling is perfectly possible in other countries, but also that it can have a 'real world' impact that today's Hollywood-centric narrative universes very infrequently do. Scolari's case study demonstrates that to fully understand the contingency of today's US/UK transmedia storytelling, scholars must attend to geographical as well as historical variation.

While the authors make a very good argument for scholarly attention to both temporal and geographical variations in the alignments from which transmedia storytelling emerges, their case studies imply that there might be general narrative principles shared by all expanded storyworlds or at least by some subsets of these storyworlds. The authors suggest all pulp fiction transmedia storytelling expanded their universes through four factors: narrative implication and narrative expansion, seriality, and retroactive linkages devised for world-building. Matthew Freeman's case study of *Superman* details how these four factors played out in the Man of Steel's transformation from comic book to transmedia hero. Paolo Bertetti's case study of *Conan the Barbarian* develops a sophisticated and elaborate narratological framework to analyse the transformations of a character across different texts and media. I am eager to see whether Bertetti's framework accounts for the myriad and often conflicting manifestations of Sherlock Holmes in media from books to television to video games. More generally, is it possible to develop a one-size fits all theory that will both illuminate the relationships between the various elements of an expanded storyworld at a particular time and account for changes over time? We will all have to do a great deal more research before this question can be answered.

Roberta Pearson
University of Nottingham

DOI: 10.1057/9781137434371.0002

Note

1 'A Case of Identity: *Sherlock*, *Elementary* and their National Broadcasting Systems' in Roberta Pearson and Anthony N. Smith, eds., *Storytelling in the Media Convergence Age: Exploring Screen Narratives* (London: Palgrave MacMillan, forthcoming).

DOI: 10.1057/9781137434371.0002

Formal Acknowledgements for Third Party Materials

Figure 3.1 is Graffiti of the *Nestornauta* by Leonardo Samarani

▶

DOI: 10.1057/9781137434371.0003

Notes on Authors

Roberta Pearson is Professor of Film and Television Studies at the University of Nottingham, UK. She has published numerous books, book chapters and journal articles. These include the edited collection, *Reading Lost: Perspectives on a Hit Television Show*, a co-authored book, *Star Trek and American Television*, and most recently the edited collection, *Storytelling in the Media Convergence Age*, coming out later this year.

▶ *Note: This book was conceived and discussed collectively. The introduction and conclusions were written together by all three authors. Chapter 1 was written by Paolo Bertetti, Chapter 2 by Matthew Freeman, and Chapter 3 by Carlos A. Scolari.*

palgrave▸**pivot**

Introduction: Towards an Archaeology of Transmedia Storytelling

Carlos A. Scolari, Paolo Bertetti and Matthew Freeman

Abstract: *The concept of transmedia storytelling was introduced by Henry Jenkins in an already seminal article published by* Technology Review *in January 2003. The chapter presents transmedia storytelling in the context of contemporary media research and describes the main academic discussions around it. Issues such as the participation of fans in the construction of transmedia narrative worlds or the media/narrative expansions are discussed in this chapter. Finally, the chapter also deals with two key concepts of the book: transmedia archaeology and transmedia pulp fiction.*

Keywords: collaborative culture; media industry; transmedia archaeology; transmedia pulp fiction; transmedia storytelling

Scolari, Carlos A., Paolo Bertetti, and Matthew Freeman. *Transmedia Archaeology: Storytelling in the Borderlines of Science Fiction, Comics and Pulp Magazines.* Basingstoke: Palgrave Macmillan, 2014. DOI: 10.1057/9781137434371.0005.

What is transmedia storytelling? The concept of transmedia storytelling was introduced by Henry Jenkins in an already seminal article published by *Technology Review* in January 2003. According to Jenkins (2003, 2006a, 2006b, 2009), many contemporary works are characterised by expanding their narrative through different media (e.g. film, television, comics, books, etc.) and other platforms (blogs, forums, wikis, social networks, etc.). For example, the Fox series *24* began as a television show but ended up including mobisodes, webisodes, video games for consoles, mobile games, comics, novels, and board games, as well as a plethora of official and fan websites. We can add a second feature to this transmedia dimension of storytelling evidenced by Jenkins: the creation of user-generated content. Transmedia narratives may begin in a Hollywood studio or in the comic book editor's office in Manhattan but continue, for example, in a blog written by a Mexican girl or in a parody video uploaded onto Youtube by a group of Australian fans (Ibrus and Scolari, 2012; Scolari, 2009a, 2013a, 2013b).

The expansion of the narrative is thus at the same time a social, commercial and semiotic necessity of certain tales. In many cases the consumers (readers, viewers, users) consider that the extension of a narrative world is not enough so they ask for more. When Arthur C. Doyle decided to kill Sherlock Holmes in the Reichenbach Falls (*The Final Problem*, 1893), the readers asked for more stories for almost a decade. The result: in 1902 Holmes returned in *The Hound of the Baskervilles* and was definitely revived in *The Adventure of the Empty House* (1903). From a commercial perspective, the expansion of a successful narrative world is one of the most popular strategies. Do people like *CSI: Las Vegas?* Then let's create *CSI: Miami* and *CSI: NY!* Finally, the expansion of a narrative world could be considered under a semiotic perspective. From this point of view, it could be said that certain narratives are asking for an expansion. The storytelling is so strong that the characters require more space and time to tell their stories. J.J. Abram's *Lost* is a good example of a complex narrative asking for more space and time (in fact, the television story was expanded into video games, novels, mobisodes and alternate reality games). In the specific case of transmedia expansions – that is, when the textual network expands to other media and platforms, like in the aforementioned example of *Lost* – it is possible to find one or two combinations of these necessities.

The second feature of transmedia storytelling is the participation of users in the extension of the narrative worlds. We could imagine a pyramid of user participation and engagement: on the base, we find

DOI: 10.1057/9781137434371.0005

the consumer of a single media product (e.g. the viewers of a television series or the readers of a comic); on the second level, the consumer of the different media products (i.e. the consumers of the transmedia narrative world expressed in different textual supports); on the third level, the fan who shares contents online and actively participates in the conversations around the narrative world; finally, on the top of the pyramid we find the prosumer: the fan who produces new contents and expands the narrative world. This is the core of the fan culture. The production of a user-generated piece of content (i.e. a parody, an alternative end, a spin-off, a fake trailer, a fake intro, a recapitulation, etc.) represents one of the highest levels of transmedia engagement.

The standard definition of transmedia storytelling thus could be represented by the following formula:

Media Industry (canon) + Collaborative Culture (fandom) = Transmedia Storytelling

This standard definition – more or less shared by scholars and professionals – may be reviewed under different perspectives. Transmedia storytelling is an interdisciplinary research object that can be analysed from different points of views. For example, from a strictly semiotic perspective, there is no difference from bottom up (fans) and top down (media industry) originated texts. From this point of view, transmedia storytelling could be considered as a network of texts in different media that expand a fictional universe. In other words, for semioticians collaborative practices could be very important in the study of transmedia but they are not necessary (nor sufficient) to define it. Many researchers – not necessarily semioticians – support this definition that privileges the intertextual narrative network. On the other hand, scholars coming from ethnography and cultural studies may privilege the activity of the users, the generation of new peripheral contents and the fan (sub)cultures. In this case, the participation of users in the extension of the narrative world is a basic component of the transmedia formula.

Another critical issue: everyone repeats that transmedia is about 'expansion'. What kind of expansion are we talking about? It is possible to identify at least two possible expansions: *media expansions* and *narrative expansions*. In the first case, the storytelling expands from one media to another (i.e. *The Walking Dead*, a story born as a comic book expanded to television and video games). In the second one, the storytelling occurs in the same medium and incorporates new characters and/or narrative events (i.e. Robin/Dick Grayson debuted in *Detective Comics* #38 / April

DOI: 10.1057/9781137434371.0005

1940, almost one year after the appearance of Batman in *Detective Comics* #27 / May 1939). In narratologic terms it could be said that the level of the story (events and worlds) are independent from the medium / semiotic system of manifestation. From this perspective the perfect case for transmedia storytelling occurs when media and narrative expansions converge into a single narrative experience.

Narrative Expansion + Media Expansion = Transmedia Storytelling

In this context transmedia storytelling could be considered a specific case of a more general transtextual storytelling. Many strategies that allow stories to cross multiple texts in the same medium quite often also work to allow stories to cross multiple media (i.e. seriality, cliffhangers, etc.). Thus theorising narrative expansions means using the same principles, be them transtextual or transmedial.

But if transmedia storytelling is about textual expansion should we then expulse from the transmedia universe textual works such as trailers, sneak-peeks and recaps? Narratives can also be compressed for the generation of snack formats. These textual pieces are also part of the transmedia narrative world so they should not be expulsed from the researcher desktop.

Finally, a reflection on transmedia and fiction. Is it possible to identify transmedia experiences beyond fiction? The answer is affirmative. Journalists have been producing transmedia storytelling for years, even before the arrival of the World Wide Web. Stories could start on the radio, continued on the television and expanded to journals. The web and the social networks just added powerful environments for user participation. Documentaries are also adopting transmedia strategies (i.e. the multiplatform productions by National Geographic that span from the traditional magazine to television and web). Transmedia storytelling is a transversal phenomenon that covers any kind of narrative. However, there are many issues concerning the nature of transmedia worlds, and particular narrative types and genres may be more suited to transmedia storytelling than others – an issue which this book considers.

I.1   Transmedia research

In the last years 'transmedia storytelling' has transformed itself into a global keyword for media professionals and researchers. Since the

DOI: 10.1057/9781137434371.0005

publication of Jenkins' seminal article in *Technology Review* in 2003, a concept born in an academic environment 'expanded' to professional and commercial circuits. From the perspective of scholars, transmedia narrative worlds are a real challenge for media researchers. Communication and media studies have always proposed monomediatic approaches. For example, there are many specific semiotics (semiotics of radio, semiotics of television, semiotics of cinema, semiotics of theatre, etc.) but we do not have a semiotics of transmedia experiences (Scolari, 2012, 2013b).

The same may be said about the political economy of transmedia: there are a lot of studies about traditional broadcasting financing strategies but understandings of transmedia practices are so new that researchers are still dealing with them.

Research on transmedia covers different territories and perspectives. On the academic side, in the Comparative Media Studies (MIT) Jenkins boosted a series of interesting Masters' dissertations in the early 2000s (Ford, 2007a; Long, 2007). The first PhD dissertation on transmedia storytelling was defended by Christy Dena in the University of Sidney (Dena, 2009). Another important reference of this first generation of studies was the monographic issue of *Convergence: The International Journal of Research into New Media Technologies* edited by Jenkins and Mark Deuze. This special issue included contributions close to that of the spirit of the present book, such as Neil Perryman's analysis of the *Doctor Who* transmedia universe (Perryman, 2008).

Researchers may approach transmedia as a general phenomenon – one that can be analysed from different perspectives –or instead may focus their intervention on specific productions. From the first perspective, we can include the narratological reflections on the status of transmedia storytelling and other textual experiences, such as intermediality (Elleström, 2010; Grishanova and Ryan, 2010; Ryan, 2004, 2005), transfictionality (Ryan, 2013), transmedial worlds (Klastrup and Tosca, 2004), or the study of fan communities and user-generated contents (Hills, 2002; Booth, 2010; Lobato, Thomas and Hunter, 2011).

From the second perspective (the analysis of specific productions), the researcher studies a single narrative universe. For example, the expanded narrative universe created around a TV series such as *Lost*, one of the most popular and classic examples of contemporary transmedia storytelling, has generated a dense corpus of academic works (Jones, 2007; Clarke, 2009; Lavery, 2009; Pearson, 2009; Scolari, 2009a). Other scholars prefer to focus on specific media: for example,

DOI: 10.1057/9781137434371.0005

there's a strong connection between transmedia storytelling and the transformations of contemporary television (Mittel, 2006; Smith, 2009; Scolari, 2009b; Evans, 2011; Clarke, 2013). This short overview of transmedia research should also include critical approaches to Jenkins' convergence culture such as those developed by Couldry (2011) and Hay and Couldry (2011).

I.2   Why an archaeology of transmedia?

Despite the growing prominence of transmedia as a keyword, most of the scientific publications about transmedia storytelling are dedicated to contemporary productions. Examples include *The Matrix, Harry Potter, The Lord of the Rings, Lost* or *Star Wars.* When scholars or professionals talk about 'old productions', they mention *Star Trek* or *Doctor Who.* But if we consider transmedia storytelling as an experience characterised by the expansion of the narrative through different media and, in many cases, by the participation of the users in that expansion, then we could say that this is not a new phenomenon. As early as the 1930s many popular narratives – such as Batman or Mickey Mouse – had been expanded to different media (comic, pulp magazines, radio, etc.). At the same time, the fan communities were very active and participated greatly in their expansion of the fictional world.

To reconstruct the origins of transmedia storytelling and to understand the evolution of these 'new' narratives formats is one of the challenges for media researchers. An archaeology of transmedia should start with the transmedia productions created before the introduction of the concept in the early 2000s and move backward, looking for transmedia storytelling practices in the past. Going back to the past means identifying textual networks, looking for textual 'fossils' and reconstructing production and consumption practices. If, according to Jenkins (2003, 2006a, 2006b, 2009), at least, transmedia storytelling emerges from a cultural convergence between media industry and collaborative practices, it could be said that the researcher has a territory to explore at least 500 years' worth of history (since Gutenberg created the first media industry: the printed book).

This book does not go so far. Instead, it serves to open the discussion about the origins of transmedia storytelling in the context of Western mass culture and presents three case studies from three different

DOI: 10.1057/9781137434371.0005

national contexts: *Conan the Barbarian*, *Superman* and *El Eternauta*.
These fictional narrative worlds, even if created in different countries
(UK, USA and Argentina respectively) and in different periods (*Conan
the Barbarian* in the 1930s, *Superman* in the 1930s and *El Eternauta* in
the 1950s), are very well-known and can be seen as representative of
the global popular culture. Thus neatly mirroring the way in which
transmedia storytelling itself spans across multiple platforms, this
book explores an archaeology of transmedia storytelling not only
across different historical periods but also across different countries
with different influences. We examine transmedia storytelling from
the diverse perspectives of varying capitalistic and political contexts,
across the midsection of the twentieth century, considering the roles of
fandom, narrative practices, and even discursive political movements
on transmedia storytelling.

Importantly, these three case studies also represent three slightly
different sub-genres: heroic fantasy, superhero and science fiction. While
each study will be shown to have expanded into a variety of other media
platforms, such as radio, cinema, cards and animation,
each were born out of a particular pulp tradition in magazines and
comics. Equally, the fans participated in the creation of new texts that
expanded the original fictional world. In understanding this archaeological approach, we emphasise the role of pulp genres and forms – defining
this corpus our 'transmedia pulp fiction'.

I.3   Defining transmedia pulp fiction

Transmedia storytelling has been defined as 'a process where integral
elements of a fiction get dispersed systematically across multiple [media]
channels for the purpose of creating a unified and coordinated entertainment experience' (Jenkins, 2011). For Jenkins, this process of unfolding
stories across multiple media platforms serves to make 'distinctive contributions to our understanding of the storyworld' – a fictional space that
is constructed in and across these multiple media (2006a, 334). But the
precise narratological means through which this may occur can actually
vary depending on the broader media landscape. In other words, while
the concept of transmedia storytelling has become mostly synonymous
with recent digital transformations in a contemporary setting – often
associated with new formats such as the webseries, for example, where

interaction is at its most pronounced – it is equally important to re-examine and synthesise more traditional media while tracing the relations between older storytelling practices and seemingly newer strategies of transmedia. This approach provides for a clearer grasp of transmedia as a trans-historical practice of media production that bridges these older and newer practices together.

On a purely narratological level, for instance, we might argue that the above description of transmedia storytelling is underpinned by attributes of storytelling that cut across historical and contemporary media alike – strategies characterised above as transtextual storytelling. Two such attributes of this are what Gregory Steirer calls narrative implication and expansion (2011). According to Steirer, narrative implication and narrative expansion are two ways that fictional storyworlds can be extended across texts. With narrative implication, 'the details of a single, self-contained story gesture to additional histories, events, characters, or locations not fully developed within the story itself' (Ibid.). 'Stories might also introduce distinctive characters with incomplete backstories' (Ibid.). Narrative implication thus implies the existence of untold stories, hinting at a larger storyworld beyond the confines of the narrative taking place – a further series of spaces where concurrent adventures are unfolding.

Narrative implication was in fact a common narratological feature of pulp fiction in the early twentieth century – the popular if maligned products of this period's fiction factories that specialised in the adventures of pulp heroes such as *The Shadow, Zorro, Tarzan*, and of course *Conan the Barbarian* (Smith, 2000, 2). Pulp magazines have a history as far back as *The Argosy* in 1882, but it was directly between the two world wars when the pulps truly flourished (Smith, 2000, 5–6). Prior to early 1931, when *The Shadow* became the sole focus of his own eponymously titled magazine, the pulps were an anthological medium, each issue built up of multiple stories and recurring characters whose popularity determined the frequency of their later re-appearance. The pulps framed their narrative style around the navigation of untold mysteries, implying to readers a larger mythology that was untold in one edition of the pulp title but was revealed across later editions. One example concerned the true identity of *The Shadow*, a crime-fighting vigilante with the psychic ability to cloud men's minds. Dressing in a black slouch hat with a crimson-lined cloak, *The Shadow* adopted multiple identities and disguises, remaining a mystery in both the hearts of his enemies and the

DOI: 10.1057/9781137434371.0005

minds of his readership. His true identity was scattered across different personas and multiple editions of magazines in the same way as Steirer (2011) suggests above, as 'the details of a single, self-contained story' [...] gesture to additional histories, events [and] characters not fully developed within the story itself'.

As hinted by the role of narrative implication on pulp storytelling, this era's pulp fiction might well be delineated as stepping stones of entertainment, a concept important for our purposes. This idea of fiction as stepping stones was implied back in 1923 by Edgar Rice Burroughs, 'perhaps the single most popular pulp writer' (DeForest, 2004, 77) and author of pulp exemplar *Tarzan of the Apes*. Burroughs offered the following analogy for the pleasures to be found in reading pulp fiction:

> My youngest boy collects empty match boxes. The fact that they are all of the same kind makes no difference to him, but in that he shows the true spirit of the collector and of the reader. The really great purpose of this fiction is, as I see it, that it is like stepping stones of entertainment. The reading of fiction motivates one's mind to flow to its next stepping stone, just like a collector of match boxes, and, lo, a new world will be opened to him. (*Los Angeles Times* 7 January 1923, 42)

The 'world' to which Burroughs alluded highlights further aspects of storytelling – each of which underpinned the influence of pulp narratology on transmedia storytelling. In ways complementing the conception of narrative implication, the first of these is the hint towards what Steirer calls narrative expansion. Readers had begun to associate the reading of narrative as that which functioned similarly as product consumption: for readers, the texts of the period grew into stepping stones of entertainment – the narrative further expanding across texts. According to Steirer, narrative expansion 'involves the expansion of a given narrative beyond the confines of a single text, usually in such a way that many of the original characters, settings, and histories are preserved and/or further developed through encounters with new characters, settings, and events' (2011). While divided according to genre – each magazine retained a clear identity as science fiction, horror, adventure and so on – pulps exploited narrative expansion by constructing story as that which continued across numerous iterations. The pulp magazine editors of the 1920s discovered that the best method for bringing readers back to the same publication from one month to the next was to narrate ongoing adventures, with each issue producing the climax for one story while pointing towards

DOI: 10.1057/9781137434371.0005

another. As demonstrated by the scattering of *The Shadow*'s identity, each issue resolved one chapter and created new ones that played out over weeks.

The narrative structure described by Burroughs and suggested in the earlier example of *The Shadow* hence involved the almost indefinite continuation of a story, serialised in such a way that it enabled the expansion of a fictional storyworld through the preservation of its settings and histories. Thus related to this conception of narrative expansion is seriality. Burroughs also hinted towards seriality in his aforementioned quote, recognising pulp storytelling as that which works like a series of stepping stones, each stone an event that leads to the next chapter – the leap between stones working like a metaphor for keeping readers hooked on what will happen next and so on and so forth.

The form of seriality underpinning transmedia storytelling is a very specific form. According to Ben Singer, seriality serves to 'extend the experience of the single text by division, with the selling of the media product in chapters, featuring an overarching story that carries over from episode to episode' (1990, 190). Yet according to Jenkins' definition, transmedia storytelling requires 'each [textual] entry [...] to be self-contained so that you do not need to have seen the film to enjoy the game, and vice versa' (2006a, 97–98). Transmedia storytelling, to adopt Smith's take on seriality, 'evokes an ongoing storyworld across a sequence of textual instalments' (2012, 8). Smith recognises storytelling as a series of stepping stones, to continue with the earlier metaphor. Steirer touches on this relationship between seriality and transmedia storytelling, noting that the former is 'indicative of narrative expansion' (2011). Sam Ford further elaborates on the role of seriality on transmedia storytelling, stating that

> Seriality has become a conscious part of creating immersive story worlds [...] these properties have a serial storytelling structure, multiple creative forces which author various parts of the story, a sense of long-term continuity, a deep character backlog, and a sense of permanence. (2007b)

While Steirer acknowledges that transmedia storytelling has thus far been 'employed in discussions of twenty-first-century (and late-twentieth-century) fiction and narrative,' it is this book's proposition that in reframing this concept in historical contexts of twentieth-century culture, an extensive pulpification of this historical period's surrounding

DOI: 10.1057/9781137434371.0005

media will be shown as that which accelerated the practice of transmedia storytelling (2011). Many – if not all – of Ford's conceptual assumptions about contemporary transmedia storytelling can be identified in the historical operations of pulp magazines, which used these same strategies of the serial story, long-term continuity, permanence, and indeed a deep character backlog. Burroughs even hinted at the relationship between storytelling, notably serial storytelling as told across multiple texts, and the building of a vast fictional world. These two narratological features in many respects best characterised the narrative tradition of the pulp magazine, founded as it was on providing readers with ongoing escapism into far-away worlds of fantasy.

A final narratological aspect intrinsic to transmedia storytelling, and one further hinted by Burroughs in relation to a very different context, is the notion of world-building. For Jenkins, world-building is 'the process of designing a fictional universe that […] is sufficiently detailed to enable many different stories to emerge but coherent so that each story feels like it fits with the others' (2006a, 335). In the 1920s, pulp editors responded to the demand for more and more story by exploring more retroactive approaches to world-building, connecting the stories of one pulp character with others to expand the storyworld and allow more stories to be told within that world. The assumption was that readers who responded positively to one story would be more easily persuaded to read a different story featuring a different hero – and thus purchase further editions of the magazine – if both sets of characters were seen to share the same fictional world, linking the exploits of one pulp hero with those of another.

Writing in direct relation to world-building, Mark J. P. Wolf describes such a strategy as a retroactive linkage, describing this strategy as that which is 'done for commercial reasons, such as when an author hopes to tie his less successful books into a popular world he has created, hoping to increase their sales' (2012, 219). Defining such a linkage, Wolf writes,

> A joining of two independently-created [fictional] worlds that previously had existed separately, usually through a character who appears in both worlds, or by the revelation that the two worlds share a [...] geographical linkage. Authors who develop multiple worlds will often link them retroactively, to compile their world-building efforts into a single entity. (2012, 380–381)

A clear example of the retroactive linkage would include a pulp serial called *At the Earth's Core*, published in *The All-Story* magazine in 1914.

DOI: 10.1057/9781137434371.0005

Here Edgar Rice Burroughs created a world called Pellucidar, a land inhabited by an intelligent species of pterodactyls called Mahars. Later entries in the series incorporated visits from Tarzan. The crossover narration was reciprocated when, in a later story titled *Tarzan and the Jewels of Opar*, published in 1916 in *The All-Story*, Tarzan stumbled across the lost civilisation discovered in *At the Earth's Core*. Burroughs' intention for his first sequel, titled *The Return of Tarzan*, was for his hero to 'encounter a strange race living in the ruins of a former great city' (20 December 1912). Correspondingly, in another of Burroughs' stories called *The Land That Time Forgot* – this time published in *Blue Book Magazine* in 1918 – readers were presented with a narrativisation of this former great city, here called Caspak, a place inhabited by dinosaurs. Caspak, as was revealed only at the end of the story, bordered the same jungle of Tarzan's adventures. Such an example constitutes world-building, providing the reader with new content relating to the geographical construction of a storyworld. This retroactive linking of Burroughs' fictions – exploiting the popularity of one work to boost the readership of his others – emerged as a common characteristic of pulp titles.

We might therefore assert that pulp fiction was characterised according to four defining narratological attributes: narrative implication and narrative expansion, seriality and retroactive linkages devised for world-building. Each of these four attributes is part of the fabric of transmedia storytelling in a more contemporary setting. Thus we can infer that certain core characteristics of what we understand as a generally contemporary media phenomenon can be seen to have worked under different circumstances in different historical periods, leading us to see where transmedia storytelling may have evolved from and from within which industrial-cultural settings. What's more, the role of user-generated content – a wider attribute of the transmedia experience in the contemporary setting – became important to such pulp titles. Fan cultures began to develop in the 1930s around science fiction conventions and memorabilia fairs, encouraging engagement between audience and producer. What, however, were the effects of pulp fiction storytelling and related audience activities on other media during and after its height of success? In which instances and for what reasons did the storytelling deployed in pulp magazines – rooted in narrative implications and expansions, serialised via retroactive linkages across texts – inform engagement strategies for transmedia storytelling across surrounding media forms?

DOI: 10.1057/9781137434371.0005

I.4   Three characters in search of a transmedia experience

In answering these questions as well as others, the first chapter takes a character-centred approach. It focuses on *Conan the Barbarian*, a fantasy hero created in the 1930s by pulp writer Robert Howard. In this chapter (written by Paolo Bertetti), working in the framework of the heroic fantasy sub-genre, we analyse the origins of *Conan the Barbarian* in relation to the early works and the building of the character's shared universe, the Hyborian Age. We focus in particular on the peculiar role of fandom in the construction of the literary Conan canon, aiming to demonstrate the presence even in the pulp era of collaborative practices between authors and readers. The second part of the chapter follows the narrative expansions of the character across different media (apocryphal novels, comics, cinema, television and games) from the first volume editions of the 1950s to the reboot of the 2000s, outlining continuities as well as transformations in the identity of the character.

The second chapter (written by Matthew Freeman) moves on to explore the superhero sub-genre, examining Superman from a storyworld-centred approach. Building on the importance of pulp fiction identified earlier and cemented in chapter 1, this chapter looks at transmedia storytelling as it had developed by the late 1930s and 1940s in American culture. The chapter examines how attributes of pulp fiction – its narrative structures, its production style and its effect on how audiences engaged with its stories – developed a common alignment between pulp magazines, comic books and strips, radio dramas and movie serials during this period. Specifically, and by using Superman and his storyworld as a case study, we consider how this alignment encouraged connections between multiple media that facilitated transmedia storytelling to intensify. Underpinning this alignment – as strategies common to pulp magazine operated across media as a form of transmedia world-building – were attributes equally applicable to both historical pulp fiction and contemporary transmedia fiction: seriality, narrative implication and expansion, and retroactive linkages.

In chapter 3 (written by Carlos Scolari), the analysis focuses on an Argentine comic published in the late 1950s: *El Eternauta* (Oesterheld and López, 1975). Argentine comic books lived their golden age in the 1950s with the success of comics for adult readers and a series of narrative mutations (such as the emergence of a new conception of the hero,

DOI: 10.1057/9781137434371.0005

now more human and collective). The chapter describes these processes and explains the origins of a fictional world that is considered a
reference in the Argentine science fiction and comic narrative. After
describing the different transmedia extensions, versions and adaptations
of *El Eternauta* produced in the last 50 years, the chapter explores the
contemporary reappropriations of the character – specifically the figure
of the *Nestornauta* – under a political perspective.

As acknowledged earlier, protesting to unveil the full history of transmedia storytelling is far beyond the scope of this book. We do not claim
to unravel the archaeology of transmedia in all its complex, discursive
alterations. But we do protest to offer an introductory book to the
archaeology of transmedia storytelling, in turn opening the door to a
new generation of future publications on the topic.

DOI: 10.1057/9781137434371.0005

1

Conan the Barbarian: Transmedia Adventures of a Pulp Hero

Paolo Bertetti

▶

Abstract: *This chapter aims to explore the transmedia fictional world of* Conan the Barbarian *from a character-centred approach. The first part of the chapter focuses on the original Conan stories published in 1930s pulp magazines and shows how some storytelling mechanisms, such as word-building or user-generated contents, usually related to contemporary transmedia storytelling, were already active in the pulp era. In the second part, we concentrate on literary and transmedia expansions of the character from the 1950s to the 1990s (with a brief look at the franchise reboot of the 2000s), analysing the consistencies and variations of Conan's identity across various media, variations and divergences that did not compromise the recognisability of the character by receivers or, to a lesser extent, their acceptance by fans.*

Keywords: *Conan the Barbarian*; heroic fantasy; narrative expansions; pulps; transmedia characters; transmedia storytelling

Scolari, Carlos A., Paolo Bertetti, and Matthew Freeman. *Transmedia Archaeology: Storytelling in the Borderlines of Science Fiction, Comics and Pulp Magazines.* Basingstoke: Palgrave Macmillan, 2014. DOI: 10.1057/9781137434371.0006.

1.1   Transmedia characters

In this chapter we have adopted a character-centred approach to the study of transmedia storytelling in line with the work of the scholars Philippe Hamon (1977) and Vincent Jouve (1992). Similar to them, instead of considering the fictional character an entity inscribed in the text itself, we see it as a semio-pragmatic effect produced by texts, the result of an interaction between text and receiver (reader or viewer), similar to other 'text effects' such as the 'reality-effect' (Barthes, 1968) or the 'world-effect' (Odin, 2000). The character is based on a reconstruction of the fictional world of the text on the part of the receiver, where the text provides information, hints, clues, signals that allow the receiver to identify an '*effet personnage*' ('character-effect'), the illusion of a unitary human figure, logically necessary for the development of the story (Hamon, 1977). The result is a sort of mental image, partly shared culturally and socially, rather than an idiosyncratic and private one. From a 'socio-semiotic' point of view, the characters are 'cultural figures' (Courtés, 1986), namely recognised entities circulating in the cultural universe. They are detectable in texts as well as in the memory and competence of the receiver, similar by their nature to folkloric motifs.

A character can be the overall result not only of a single text, but also of a diverse series of texts, producing a semiotic object 'that finds its own being or "making sense" in a wider socio-cultural dimension, including transtextual and transmedia changes and intersemiotic translations' (Marrone, 2003, 25–26). This forming of a character from texts and between different texts is similar to Levi-Strauss' idea of myth, which is never completely enclosed in a single text. It is the case of legendary heroes (such as those of the old German legends) or the modern serial and transmedia characters, ranging from familiar classics such as *Tarzan* and *Zorro* to *Harry Potter* or, in our case, *Conan the Barbarian*. From this perspective, then a 'transmedia character' is a fictional hero whose adventures are told across different media forms, each one giving more detail about the life of the character.[1]

In my opinion, the concept of a transmedia character is not simply one notion among others related to transmedia storytelling. I see it rather as the platform for a genuinely different logic of construction of transmedia, which merges with the logic of transmedia storytelling, as intended by Jenkins (2006a). It centres on the idea of a shared, fictional (or diegetic) world. For Jenkins, world-building is a key concern of

DOI: 10.1057/9781137434371.0006

transmedia storytelling; every text of a franchise extends storytelling by exploring different aspects of the shared world and showing different courses of action, such as by focusing on events that were only sketched in the primary ('mothership') text.

This world-centred logic is typical of the more recent transmedia productions, to which – not surprisingly – Jenkins (2006a) only refers. I believe conversely that transmedia is not simply a phenomenon that has emerged in recent years on account of technological convergence but rather one that can be traced back almost to the origins of the modern cultural industry between the end of the 1800s and 1900s. We could say that older forms of transmedia franchises were constructed on character sharing rather than on the logics of a particular world. In this regard Scott (2009) introduces the notion of the character-oriented franchise, tracing the origins of transmedia productions as far back as the age of silent movies, identifying economic and promotional strategies common to contemporary media franchises. Even Jenkins (2009), harking back to the topic, seems to suggest a similar idea:

> We might well distinguish Felix [the Cat] as a character who is extracted from any specific narrative context (given each of his cartoons is self-contained and episodic) as opposed to a modern transmedia figure who carries with him or her the timeline and the world depicted on the 'mother ship,' the primary work which anchors the franchise. As I move through this argument, I will connect transmedia to earlier historical practices, trying to identify similarities and differences along the way.

Actually, fictional worlds (transmedia or otherwise) and fictional characters are not consistent. With the exception of some special cases, such as Robinson Crusoe, fictional worlds are generally inhabited by a multitude of characters (are 'multipersonal'; see Dolezel, 1998), and the different stories that are told in these shared universes may focus on any one of them. Conversely, one particular character may appear in different narrative worlds. In fact, this character may appear in totally different narrative settings according to the story being told. But, even though the different incarnations of one character share a common setting, it does not necessarily follow that they share a common fictional world. From a semiotic perspective, a fictional possible world is not only a possible state of things, or a set of objects and individuals provided with properties, but also a set of action predicates that define a given course of events (Eco, 1979, 131). It is therefore possible to say that transmedia storytelling

DOI: 10.1057/9781137434371.0006

does not simply comprise of a shared world, but also of an *acted* shared world (Bertetti, 2014). If the fictional world also includes transformations acted within it, then the concept of narrative coherence becomes a central topic (Jenkins, 2006a). In fact, on the basis of counterfactual logic (Eco, 1979), every different course of action inevitably engenders a different possible world. This is exactly what occurs in many character-oriented franchises, where the character's nature and the storylines contrast with predecessors as they are rewritten and move from one medium to another. *Conan the Barbarian*, as we will see, is an exemplary case of study.

1.2   Barbarian genesis

Conan the Barbarian is definitely a popular figure in mass culture, as evidenced by the variety of media productions featuring him: movies, online RPG, comic books, novels, television series, and so on. For many his most famous incarnation is still the muscular warrior played by Arnold Schwarzenegger in the film directed by John Milius more than 30 years ago; for others it is the savage barbarian in Frank Frazetta's illustrations, an out-and-out icon for generations of Heavy Metal fans.

Actually the Conan story goes back much further, making him one of mass culture's most popular and long-lasting creations. His origins are rooted in the rich humus of pre-war pulp magazines. He made his first appearance in 'The Phoenix on the Sword' which was included in a December 1932 issue of *Weird Tales*, one of the most legendary magazines of the pulp era. Specialising in fantasy and horror fiction, *Weird Tales* was well known for having published many of H.P. Lovecraft's tales.

Conan's creator was Robert E. Howard, a prolific Texan pulp fiction writer. Born in 1906, he devoted his short life (he died by his own hand on June 11, 1936) to writing for many different genres: oriental adventures, noir, western, sport fiction (mainly about the boxing world, which he knew well from his success as an amateur boxer), historical fiction and even romantic fiction. But he was most famous for his fantasy writing.[2]

During the last part of his life, Howard published 16 Conan tales and the novel *The Hour of the Dragon*. A further four complete stories were found among his papers after his death. These were published posthumously in the 1950s and 1960s. Three unfinished stories were also discovered, one of which is set in Conan's world, where he plays only

DOI: 10.1057/9781137434371.0006

a minor role. Howard also sketched the plot for a fourth story as well as writing a pseudo-historical essay, 'The Hyborian Age', in which the author outlines the history and geography of Conan's imaginary world. This was also published posthumously.[3]

Howard is often considered to be the father of heroic fantasy (or sword and sorcery), a kind of fantasy adventure fiction. These stories are often set in exotic or imaginary medieval-like kingdoms (Howard preferred to write about the former) where the magic prevails. Sword and sorcery stories usually focus on a sword-wielding hero who faces supernatural perils. Unlike literary works of high fantasy, such as J.R.R. Tolkien's *The Lord of the Rings* or C.S. Lewis's *Chronicles of Narnia* that bring together chivalric adventures, fairytale traditions and myth, chivalric and fairytale elements play a less important role in heroic fantasy. Here the emphasis is on action and adventure, and sources of inspiration are less likely to be the Arthurian legends or Nordic and Celtic mythologies. Inspiration for the new genre can be found in the work of popular romance writers like H. Ridder Haggard and Talbot Mundy, who experimented with an exciting blend of history and adventure, exoticism and magic. Lord Dunsany's fantasy tales, published at the beginning of the last century, and A. Merrit's *The Ship of Ishtar* (1924) were also key influences. Planetary romances such as the Martian Novels by the earlier cited Edgar Rice Burroughs (whose first, *Under the Moons of Mars*, came out in 1912) were also important in helping to define the distinctive traits of the sub-genre. If we overlook their weak rationalisation and setting on an alien planet, their narrative situations and figurative imagery have a lot in common with those of the incoming sword and sorcery writing.

Howard's *The Shadow Kingdom* (1929) is conventionally regarded as being the first heroic fantasy story – at least in America (Tompkins, 2006). Its heroic main character is King Kull of Valusia. Although similar to Conan in many ways, Kull did not achieve the level of popularity that was awaiting Conan. Both are barbarian mercenaries who become rulers of a great civilised nation in a mythical proto-historic world in the aftermath of a military coup d'état. *The Phoenix on the Sword* was actually a rewrite of the unsold King Kull story, *By This Axe I Rule*. In it Howard changed the main character, the setting and a few scenes, turning the focus onto action and supernatural elements (Louinet, 2003). Nevertheless, the two characters have a lot in common, but while Kull is a thoughtful and troubled character, Conan fills his tales with dynamic

DOI: 10.1057/9781137434371.0006

adventure. From a semiotic point of view this genesis is interesting, as it shows that the identity of a character, at least in popular literature, depends only up to a certain point on his *doing* (i.e. his deeds). The same story can be told with either Conan or Kull in the leading role, and the construction of the character is in many ways the result of transforming and recombining properties and attributes of a figurative kind. As if to say that, regardless of Vladimir Propp (1958), the distinction between constants (functions) and variables (attributes of dramatis personae) was clearly present in the productive practice of popular writers.

As with Kull, Conan is an outstanding and distinctive character, at least compared to most of the fictional characters from the pulp era (as well as some of his later transpositions). Despite his savagery and roughness, his absolute trust in strength and the sword, Conan is not a wicked person. Of course, he steals and kills, but he does so according to a personal, barbaric code of honour. He is loyal to his friends and respects the valour and nobility of the enemy; he is neither deceptive nor sneaky. Unlike a lot of adventure fiction, the Conan stories written by Howard are not based on the classic Manichaeism between good and evil: the Conan tales are essentially about a different kind of contrast. The theme explored is that of the barbarian who comes into contact (or rather clashes) with a more ancient and refined civilisation, and it rests 'on the opposition between the innocent man (and yet not integrated into his world: the Barbarian, the pariah) and a society that appears corrupt and incomprehensible to him' (Lippi, 1989, 6).

Besides the style of the stories and the nature of their main character, what really differentiates the Conan and Kull series is their setting. Although both characters inhabit imaginary kingdoms, the Conan stories occur in a much larger, richer and more fascinating fictional world during the mythical Hyborian Age. This is a sort of imaginary proto-history that Howard placed 12,000 years in the past, 'between the years when the ocean swallowed Atlantis and the gleaming cities, and the years of the rise of the Sons of Aryas', as told in the *Nemedian Chronicles*, the *pseudobiblion* quoted in the opening of *The Phoenix on the Sword*.[4]

The Hyborian Age is actually a patchwork of many different ages and regions, a sort of giant Disneyland where a myriad of possible scenarios for adventure stories coexist. Its fabulous kingdoms and their names conjure up very different eras and civilisations: Stygia, for example, is a fantastic and fictional version of ancient Egypt; Shem corresponds to biblical Palestine; Vendhya is the mysterious India of oriental adventure

DOI: 10.1057/9781137434371.0006

stories; Brythunia resembles Early Medieval Britain; Turan roughly corresponds to the Ottoman Empire (in fact it was founded by nomads of the steppes, the Hyrkanians, as did the ancestors of the Turks) and so on. Sometimes there is a certain syncretism: for example, while Aquilonia corresponds in some ways to post-Carolingian France, it also reminds us of the Roman Empire; and the wild population of the Picts, while perhaps referring to the pre-Celtic inhabitants of Scotland of the same name, actually have much in common with the Iroquois Indians of frontier novels (Sammon, 2007).

Howard's primary references are not historical epochs and cultures that he has transfigured fantastically, but rather conventional versions handed down by earlier adventure novels and films. The building bricks of his world are stereotypical configurations, which – beginning with their name – are already well known to the reader and appeal to his encyclopaedic competence (Eco, 1984). The reader feels a sense of familiarity with this unreal world (Shanks, 2013), accompanied by a strong suggestive and evocative effect that ultimately stems from the activation of intertextual genre scripts during the act of reading these texts (Eco, 1979).

Creating a shared fictional universe for his protagonists (Conan, Kull, the Celtic chief Bran Mac Morn and others, albeit in different epochs) was clearly important to Howard, as he spent a considerable time developing it. The numerous notes on Hyborian characters and settings, as well as the maps he drew up for his personal use, testify to this. But it is perhaps the four different versions of the essay 'The Hyborian Age' that demonstrate Howard's dedication to the process of world-building, a process that lasted at least six years (Shanks, 2013, 18). As is well known, one of the central features of fantasy writing is the creation of a 'secondary world' (Tolkien, 1964), which happened long before the current tendency of building fictional worlds. As with science-fiction writing, world-creating genres depend on the creation of detailed worlds that serve as a bedrock for inner (fictional) references (Eco, 1979; Ronen, 1994; Dolezel, 1998).

1.3   The role of fandom in the construction of Conan canon

Conan is an uncommon and interesting case in which the role of fandom has been decisive in the bottom-up construction of the identity of a

DOI: 10.1057/9781137434371.0006

fictional character. It must be said that the distances separating the world of science fiction, fantasy fans and professionalism were very small in the 1930s and 1940s (Moskowitz, 1989; Pohl, 1978). Curiously, according to Frederic Pohl (1978, 17–19), the origins of organised science-fiction fandom, apart from the small correspondence clubs dotted here and there, can be traced back to a top-down initiative on the part of Hugo Gernsback (previously founder of the first SF pulp, *Amazing Stories*), when he created the Science Fiction League to increase readership of his new magazine *Wonder Stories*. Moreover, many writers (Isaac Asimov, Ray Bradbury and Pohl himself), editors (Judith Merril) and publishers (Donald Wollheim) of the so-called Golden Age of Science Fiction had previously been fans. This was also the case for Charles D. Hornig who founded *The Fantasy Fan* (1933–1934), the first fan magazine dedicated to Weird Fiction and Fantasy. Shortly after the release of the first issue of his creation, Gernsback called him up to direct *Wonder Stories*. Despite being an amateur production *The Fantasy Fan* published a number of professional authors, including H.P. Lovecraft, C.A. Smith and Robert Bloch, and even a Conan story written by Howard: *The Frost Giant's Daughter*. Perhaps on account of a near rape scene in the story, this tale was rejected by *Weird Tales*. A revised version did, however, appear in *The Fantasy Fan* with the title *Gods of the North*. The protagonist's name was also changed to Amra of Akbitana.

However, the importance of fandom in the development of the character of Conan lies not only in the publication of a rejected story. The Conan story is, in fact, an unusual one (or at least one of the first) where user-generated content became the basis of the canon of the character. The original Conan stories have no internal chronological order. Howard wrote each of them to stand alone as separate adventures. The first two Conan tales published recount the adventures of a mature leader on the throne of Aquilonia, while the following tales feature the hero at different times of his life. It is, therefore, almost certain that Howard had no precise timeline or chronology in mind when writing or drafting the earliest Conan stories (Waterman, 2014). He more than likely had the vague idea of an aging barbarian warrior who enlists into the army of Aquilonia as a mercenary after a long string of travels and adventures. After working his way up the ranks, he then becomes king of Aquilonia, the greatest nation of the Hyborian Age.

In a letter to the fan writer Peter Schuyler Miller, Howard himself said he does not follow a definite plan when writing the Conan stories, but only the inspiration of the moment:

DOI: 10.1057/9781137434371.0006

In writing these yarns I've always felt less as creating them than as if I were simply chronicling his adventures as he told them to me. That's why they skip about so much, without following a regular order. The average adventurer, telling tales of a wild life at random, seldom follows any ordered plan, but narrates episodes widely separated by space and years, as they occur to him.[5]

In 1936, P.S. Miller and J.D. Clarke, two fans, wrote the first Conan chronology in a work entitled 'A Probable Outline of Conan's Career'. It was based on the 17 Conan stories published up to that point. Miller sent a draft of the essay to Howard shortly before his death. Howard was pleased with the idea and endorsed the reconstruction of the Conan timeline in the letter quoted earlier. After making some corrections and additions, the revised chronology was published two years later in *The Hyborian Age* (Miller and Clarke, 1938).

The timeline was updated in the 1950s by Lyon Sprague de Camp to include all the Conan stories published posthumously. In the 1960s it became the basis of the Lancer chronological edition of Conan adventures and was subsequently adopted by the copyright holders, Conan Properties, Inc. (CPI), as the 'official' Conan character chronology to be followed by the Marvel Comics' transposition and subsequent apocryphal novels.

According to this reconstruction, Conan was born on the battlefield during fierce combat between his tribe and a horde of raiding Vanir. He received his baptism of blood at the age of 15 during the siege of Venarium, an outpost of Aquilonia in Cimmerian territory. Later he joined a band of Aesir (inhabitants of the north, ancestors of the Scandinavians). During a raid he was captured and taken as a slave to Hyperborea, a dark kingdom north-east of Cimmeria. He manages to escape and heads for the rich and civilised countries of the south. At the age of 17 he finds himself in the city of Zamora, where he earns a living as a thief. In the following years, he moves throughout the Hyborian lands in search of fortune, travelling from the West Coast Nations to the Black Kingdoms in the south and eastwards to Vendhya. His various professions at this time include robber, pirate, mercenary, buccaneer and soldier, according to circumstances. At the age of 38 Conan finally enlists as a scout in the Aquilonian army and takes part in operations against the wild Picts. The barbarian rises through the ranks of the Aquilonian army and soon becomes general. When the kingdom's barons revolt against the corrupt and inept King Numedides, Conan seizes his chance, kills Numedides on his throne and becomes the king of Aquilonia. He rules wisely for

DOI: 10.1057/9781137434371.0006

many years, often being called to defend his kingdom from foreign and internal enemies. His duties as king see him venturing into far corners of the world: to Khitai and Hyrkania, and the regions beyond, and even to a nameless continent in the western hemisphere.

The official chronology has been brought into question in recent years by fans (Waterman, 2014) owing to the misplacement of some of the Conan stories, primarily the posthumously published tales and fragments, whose positioning along the timeline was inevitably arbitrary. It is not by chance, therefore, that de Camp was compelled to make some adjustments, and even edit the unpublished tales by Howard (especially *The Treasure of Tranicos*) to avoid chronological inconsistencies.[6] In 1997, Joe Marek first made some suggestions for a revised timeline,[7] but it was Dale Rippke (2003) who developed the new, more coherent chronology of the life of Conan, that was adopted for the Dark Horse comic books adaptation.

Reconstructing a Conan chronology on the basis of the works by Howard, for the reasons said earlier, actually seems rather unrealistic and even bizarre, but, it was, of course, a fun game for fans. In it the life of a fictional character is to be considered real, and it subsequently becomes the object of historical and philological exercises, similar to the Great Game played by Sherlock Holmes fans. Howard himself returned repeatedly to this game when working on his pseudo-historical essay 'The Hyborian Age', where he reconstructed the events of that fabulous pre-historical age. It is also an interesting game from a semiotic point of view, as it is based on an intentional overlapping of the world of the story and the real world, challenging the fictional pact between text and reader, and ultimately the assumption of the ontological existence of a possible fictional world (Eco, 1979, 1994, 75–116). But it is also a game with remarkable practical and economic consequences.

Firstly, as Waterman (2014) notes, a character chronology focuses the reader on the *character* instead of the author or the single stories; in this sense, its reconstruction (moreover if it is made by a person other than the original author, as in our case) is the starting point of a process that tends to transform the character into a social object of inter-individual construction and public debate, rendering it independent of texts in which it was born. It was really the Miller/Clarke chronology that became the starting point for an economic exploitation of the character. It led to, and perhaps justified, the creation of new stories based on the life of Conan, beginning with the first fan fiction novel by Björn Nyberg

DOI: 10.1057/9781137434371.0006

in the 1950s and continuing with the long series of apocryphal novels of the 1980s and 1990s.

Between 1950 and 1954, Gnome Press, a small publishing house specialising in fantasy literature and science fiction, republished the whole Howard's Hyborian Cycle in a series of five hardcover books (edited by L.S. de Camp). They included the only three stories of King Kull then known (originally published in *Weird Tales* in the 1920s) and three unpublished Conan stories.

The success of the five books prompted de Camp and Gnome Press to publish two more volumes of Conan adventures: the first, *Tales of Conan* was a collection of four previously unpublished stories by Howard. Originally they had been tales of oriental adventure with medieval and modern settings. Now de Camp turned them into Conan stories, freely rewriting settings and names and adding supernatural elements. The second, *The Return of Conan*, is a good example of the thin line that separates bottom-up from top-down creativity. This is, in fact, an apocryphal novel written by a Swedish fan, Björn Nyberg, who sent the manuscript to de Camp, who revised and published it as book six of the series, coming to be part of the canon of the character. As such it was reprinted in the Lancer paperback edition of the Conan saga with the new title *Conan the Avenger*.

A new edition of the Conan stories, comprising a total of 12 volumes, was published between 1966 and 1977. This is the edition that made Conan a household name. It was edited by de Camp and the writer Lin Carter and brought all existing Conan stories (including the Nyberg novel and the posthumous collaborations previously published by Gnome books) under one roof in chronological order to form a complete account of Conan's life. De Camp and Carter linked the stories with short introductions and wrote several new episodes (it even included three brand new novels), sometimes (but not always) developing notes found in Howard's writings. Similar to present-day modes of developing transmedia narrative *expansions*, they are *interstitial microstories* (Scolari, 2009a) which fill the gaps in the *macrostory* given by the original Conan stories and the Miller/Clarke chronology approved by Howard. Despite the presence of a substantial amount of spurious material (more than half of the stories were not actually written by Howard) and the lack of philological consistency, the Lancer edition remained the reference edition of the cycle for many years, thus constituting the canon of the Conan character. In this sense, Conan differs from most literary serial characters, whose

DOI: 10.1057/9781137434371.0006

canon is strictly fixed and based on a sharp distinction between original and apocryphal stories. For example, the canon of Sherlock Holmes comprises the 56 short stories and 4 novels written by Sir Arthur Conan Doyle. Conversely, the Batman character is in some respects similar to Conan in that he 'has no primary urtext set in a specific period, but rather existed in a plethora of equally valid texts appearing constantly over more than five decades' (Uricchio and Pearson, 1991, 184).

In editing the expanded Lancer edition, de Camp and Carter profoundly altered the serial nature of the Conan cycle. As we said, Howard had no intention of writing a complete and coherent life history of Conan: the original Conan stories are, in fact, a good example of what Umberto Eco calls a *flashback-series* (or *loop-series*) 'in which the character is not followed along in a straight line during the course of his life, but is continually rediscovered at different moments of his life, obsessively revisited in order to find new opportunities for new narratives' (Eco, 1985, 168).[8] With their work, conversely, de Camp and Carter turn the series into a *saga*, a form of narrative repetition in which there is 'a continuous lineage [and] the character is followed from birth to death' (Eco, 1985, 169).

This is also the aim of further texts the two authors wrote in the late 1970s for a new series of Conan adventures. Here we find a series of properly 'apocryphal' novels by various writers that were added to the volumes of the 'official' Lancer edition. The first six were published between 1978 and 1982 by Bantam Books[9] and were closely related to the Lancer volumes of the 'Conan Saga'. In a way they filled in the missing pieces in the story. This was particularly true for the first two books, written by de Camp and Carter: *Conan the Swordsman* and *Conan the Liberator*. The second is particularly interesting because we learn for the first time how Conan conquered the throne of Aquilonia.

In the wake of the film's success, Tor Books published a long series of 42 novels between 1982 and 1997. It was written by various authors, the best known of which being Robert Jordan and Harry Turtledove, and included a novelisation of the second movie, *Conan the Destroyer*. The novels are generally quite faithful to de Camp's Conan Saga if not to the spirit of Howard's stories. This is due to the fact that Conan Properties (the company founded by the heirs and the literary agent of Howard, holder of the copyright on the character) always laid down stringent guidelines for authors: they had to respect the official chronology and avoid contradictions with previously published episodes, including any

DOI: 10.1057/9781137434371.0006

apocryphal work. Furthermore contagion between genres, pastiches, satirical or humorous narratives, and any modes of discourse out of line with the tradition of the character, at least as re-interpreted by de Camp, were forbidden.

The character of Conan thus became a sort of collective construction (Bertetti, 2011) or a 'cultural production' (Prida, 2013). The 'canon' itself is nowadays largely independent of its original author, owing much of his character to the work of de Camp as opposed to Howard. Later we will see how Roy Thomas and John Milius also played a part in his creation. The Cimmerian has become a real 'socio-semiotic hero' (Marrone, 2003), a common heritage of mass culture (or, at least, of a relatively wide number of authors and beneficiaries); a heritage that needs to be safeguarded to prevent his identity from inevitably drifting away from the original.

1.4   Transmedia adventures

Unfortunately, Conan Properties was unable to keep the contents of this diegetic universe under control as it passed into different media bands: comics in the 1970s, cinema in the 1980s and television in the 1990s. Whatever the media, however, Conan stories are always set in the Hyborian Age, even if the live action television serial used backgrounds and toponyms that would have been unfamiliar in the universe Howard conceived. However, as previously noted, a fictional world is not only a state of things or a common setting, but also a combination of transformations acted within it. From this point of view, Conan's different media incarnations do not constitute a unique fictional world. In effect, only the Conan 'mothership' (Jenkins, 2006a) (i.e. the original tales written by Howard) refers to the same world (this is also partially true of his incarnation in comics), but the other media platforms do not.

The first transmedia expansion of Conan was into comics. In October 1970, the Marvel Comics Group published the first issue of *Conan the Barbarian*. The script was written by Roy Thomas (who wrote most texts for the series) accompanied by wonderful artwork by Barry Windsor Smith. John Buscema later took over illustrating the stories. His style was perhaps better suited to describing the Howardian universe. Buscema and Frank Frazetta (the cover illustrator of the Lancer volumes) are

DOI: 10.1057/9781137434371.0006

the two artists who are probably most responsible for giving Conan his visual identity.

The different issues told the history of the barbarian. Starting with his youth in the ice lands of the North, they followed the chronology established by Miller and Clarke. The series preserved the original features of Howard's creation quite well, partly because Conan Properties imposed the same guidelines on the comic book scriptwriters as it did on the authors of the apocryphal novels. Despite these constraints, the range of his adventures was expanded excessively, causing the series to suffer. Transpositions of the original Conan tales were, in fact, alternated with adaptations of stories originally written by Howard, but featuring different characters. These included new episodes and even the transposition of works by other authors, such as *Flame Winds* by Norwell Page (1939), that introduced characters and situations directly inspired by Conan and his universe. The continuous expansion of the Conan macrostory and an ever-increasing proliferation of episodes over the years nullified any general narrative pattern, and continuity, which had been strictly controlled in the early days by Marvel, suffered greatly. What is particularly interesting for our purposes is that even though Conan Properties imposed the same rules regarding coherence to books and comics, they only applied to each specific medium. In fact, literary and comic-book expansions both began as macrostories based on the canon established by the Lancer volumes, but they were totally independent of one another, and could even contrast with each other.

In 1974 Marvel published a new large-format, black-and-white series aimed at a more adult reader, *The Savage Sword of Conan*. It was written by Roy Thomas, and the first 60 issues were drawn by John Buscema. The stories did not have a strong underlying continuity, but the quality of the series was good and it hosted numerous adaptations of the original Howard stories. But, of more interest to us here is the colour series, *King Conan* (later *Conan the King*). Published between 1980 and 1989 for a total of 55 issues, this series reveals a previously unknown side of the Conan character. In these stories Conan is both King, married to Queen Zenobia, and a family man who dedicates much of his time to bringing up his children.[10]

Although this series outlines a character who is in many respects quite different from Howard's original Conan, the course of events does not differ fundamentally from the canonic one; Zenobia was in fact created by Howard to be Conan's bride in *The Hour of the Dragon*. *King Conan*

DOI: 10.1057/9781137434371.0006

instead explores some ideas de Camp sketched in his stories dedicated to a mature and regal Conan, such as *Conan of Aquilonia*. It is here that we first meet Conn, Conan's eldest son and heir to the throne.

A truly alternative storyline appears only when the character appears on screen. In the 1980s, two Conan movies were made, both produced by Dino De Laurentis and starring the actor Arnold Schwarzenegger in the leading role. The first, *Conan the Barbarian*, was directed by John Milius; the second, *Conan the Destroyer*, much less interesting and less successful, was written by Roy Thomas and Jerry Conway, and directed by Richard Fleischer. John Milius's film of Conan's childhood and youth wanders from the canonical version of the Conan story. According to Howard and the canon, Conan grew up in Cimmeria and left his native land at the age of 19, heading for the civilised southern kingdoms in search of fortune, whereas in Milius's epic vision Conan is reduced to slavery with all his tribe when he is a child and grows up as a slave. He then becomes a powerful gladiator before becoming a free man. Following de Camp's lead, Milius transforms the whole story into a sort of Bildungsroman. The first part of the film focuses on the hero's 'development' through a series of tests; the second tells the story of him seeking his revenge against Thulsa Doom, the sorcerer who killed his parents and destroyed his village. This involves, as we will see, a sharp change in the character's nature, giving a strong motivation to his deeds, which was very untypical of Howard's Conan.

Further alternative storylines, based on different courses of action, can be found in the television series (two animated and a live action one) of the 1990s. The first animated series, *Conan the Adventurer* (65 episodes each 22 minutes long, ran from 12 September 1992 to 22 November 1993). It shows a new version of Conan's childhood, which differs both from Howard's and Milius's version. In the first episode the evil Serpent Man wizard, Wrath-Amon, transforms the whole of Conan's family into living stone in an attempt to take possession of the Star Metal Conan's father employs to forge swords. His subsequent adventures take us on a long journey as he scours Hyboria in search of a cure for his family and a way of delivering the population from Wrath-Amon's wicked rule. The series depicts Conan as a positive hero surrounded by many differ-ent supporting characters. Despite the fact that the series includes some adaptations of Howard's stories, notably *The Frost Giant's Daughter*, the spirit is closer to the comic book themes rather than that in Howard's original stories.

DOI: 10.1057/9781137434371.0006

The second animated series, *Conan and the Young Warriors* (a total of 13 episodes broadcast in 1994) was a spin-off of the earlier series. In this series Conan is a mature man who has the task of training and protecting a trio of new young warriors destined to rule over Hyboria. He teaches them 'the Road of the Warrior'. Nothing could be further from the original Conan character.

The live action television Series, *Conan the Adventurer* (22 episodes that originally ran from 1997 to 1998 in the US), stars German Bodybuilder Ralf Möller as Conan. This poor quality, low-budget production was badly directed and built around what can only be described as rather lame storylines (mainly written by Charles Henry Fabian). The episodes take their inspiration from the films rather than from Howard's stories or Marvel's comic books, but lack any narrative continuity. Once again the storyline is quite different: Conan has become a sort of Robin Hood-like figure, fighting the same villain in each episode, the evil Wizard-King HissaZul, and his band of unlikely companions (Otli, a comical dwarf; Vulkar, a Viking-like warrior and Zzeben, an agile mute). In the pilot (freely adapted from Howard's 'The Tower of the Elephant'), Conan escapes from slavery and acquires the magic Sword of Atlantis at the end of a series of trials. He then has a vision of his god, Crom, who announces that he is the one chosen to bring divine justice to Earth.

Even from this rapid overview of the transmedia expansions of Conan,[11] it emerges that his overall identity is the result of clearly independent and frequently incoherent narrative extensions. In effect, the transtextual identity of a character cannot always be defined unequivocally (Bertetti, 2011); however, what is important is that the character can be recognised by the reader. As Marrone (2003) also points out, recognisability does not seem compromised, to some extent, by the possible changes, even if they conflict with each other: the culturally recognised identity of the character is given by the set of its occurrences, and the possible existence of differences within the corpus is generally accepted. Although a sort of priority to the original ur-character is generally given, it does not necessarily follow that the character's image sedimented in popular culture is that of the original character. Some fans will therefore consider occurrences more canonical, while others will see a freer and more creative interpretation of the original. This is because the definition of characters in the sense of cognitive semantics has a prototypical nature (Rosh, 1978; Geeraerts, 1989): the identity of characters is a fuzzy concept, and some of its occurrences are more typical than others.

DOI: 10.1057/9781137434371.0006

On this basis I proposed (Bertetti, 2011) a model to help analyze the possible changes in identity to a character in different texts and media. This model, which has been used for an in-depth analysis of Conan's features, can only briefly be summarised here.

Taking up the classical Aristotelian dichotomy between *action* and *character*, namely between character as *being* and character as *doing* (a dichotomy we are able to find, 'mutatis mutandis', in contemporary semiotics, particularly in Greimas' distinction between *actants* and *actors*),[12] we can begin by distinguishing two different types of identity:

1 *existential identity*
2 *fictional identity*

These two different kinds of identity correspond to the two main textual levels according to Greimas' generative trajectory of meaning: discursive level and semio-narrative level. So we could also speak, respectively, of *discursive identity* and *semio-narrative identity*.

Existential identity is divided into

A) *Proper identity*, which is the set of elements forming the identity that relate to the being in itself of the character (we can also speak of *semantic identity*).

It can be further divided into

i) a *figurative identity*, consisting of all figurative attributes (according to Greimas) of the character (appearance, qualities etc.), including his proper name (Barthes, 1970) and his proper image, that is, the image that allows the recipient to identify a character and distinguish it from other characters (Tomasi, 1988, 26). Conan's figurative identity is relatively stable, with few variations. The best-known figurativisation is that of Schwarzenegger's muscular body as it appeared in the 1980s movies, a little excessive perhaps, but basically coherent with the traditional image established by Frazetta and Buscema. However an alternative, less titanic and more athletic figurativisation of the hero exists – see the *Weird Tales*' covers by Margareth Brundage and some of the work by new Dark Horse Comics illustrators.[13]

ii) a *thematic identity*, related to the thematic roles (a term that Greimas uses to define abstract roles such as social, familiar or cultural roles, etc.; i.e. 'warrior', 'fisherman', 'father', 'barbarian', etc.). The thematic identity refers to the set of roles a character plays, simultaneously or in succession, within a text or a series of texts. In Howard's writings Conan plays many different thematic roles at the *local level* of the single stories (Thief, Pirate, King, Mercenary, etc.), but is highly consistent at the *general level* of the series: Conan is a Barbarian, and all his features (physical, moral, character) derive from his being a Cimmerian. Expansions in different media, however, tend to turn him into a more canonical Warrior-like figure. In Milius's movie, essentially a coming-of-age story that converts the instinctive barbarian fighter into a hero, we meet a self-disciplined Conan endowed with a new skill set that includes, at least in part, training skills as well as an understanding and acceptance of a martial mystique ('the secret of steel'). The 'warrior' theme instead rises to the fore in the television series and cartoons, where Conan has become an almost trivial and traditional good hero whose barbaric origins are purely incidental.

B) *Relational identity* (or syntactic *identity*), which is based on the character's relationship with the world around him: primarily relations of space and time (temporal and spatial relations) and, secondly, relations with the other characters in the stories (*actorial relations*). A character's identity may be, to a greater or smaller extent, *relationally strong* or *relationally weak*, depending on whether the character has strong bonds with their specific fictional world (as is the case with *sitcoms*) or not. Robert Howard's Conan is a relationally weak character: he is a solitary hero, whose adventures are always set in different locations within the Hyborian World and at different times of his life. However, we should observe that Conan's identity status does change depending on the medium; in the television series and cartoons of the 1990s, we find the same setting and a recurring group of side characters.

Meanwhile, within the *narrative identity,* we can distinguish:

C) a *modal identity*, based on the character's different modalisations. In linguistics 'the term modalization relates to the procedure whereby a descriptive statement is modified by means of modal expressions' (Martin and Ringham, 2000, 87). In the narrative grammar of Greimas the term specifically refers to a set of features that define motivations and skills of the subject in relation to its doing: *wanting* (or *having to*), *being able*, *knowing* (Greimas, 1983). Conan's identity, in the course of his transmedia history, shows two different modal organisations, corresponding to two different thematisations mentioned earlier: 'barbarian' and 'warrior'. In Howard, as we said, all Conan's features (physical, psychological, intellectual, etc.) arise from his barbaric nature. His Cimmerian birth and origins determine who he is. In terms of narrative semiotics, he is an intrinsically competent subject: the barbarian that appears at the end of his adolescence in the civilised Hyborian lands is already full-fledged, and it will remain basically unchanged throughout all his later adventures. Over the years he will gain more experience, learning more and more about the civilised world, and he will acquire specific skills related to his deeds in each single story, but these will not change him significantly as he wanders his existential path. In semiotic terms, he acquires *local competences* (at episode level), but his *general competences* (in terms of series) are given once and for all. However, much of the later narrative expansion shows many relevant differences in Conan's *modal identity*. As we learned, de Camp and Milius transformed the Conan saga into a sort of Bildungsroman; moreover by introducing the theme of revenge, Milius invests Conan's *doing* with a strong motivation. The *wanting* in Howard's Conan is constitutionally weak, and derives, once again, from his barbaric nature: there is no deep and inclusive (personal or ideological) motivation to his deeds other than seeking his fortune, fighting for survival and living it up.[14] A further differentiation can be found in the live action television series, where Conan is driven not (or not only) by his *wanting,* but rather by a *having to do*: he is the one chosen by Crom, thus doomed to be 'king by his own hand' and bring back justice to Earth.[15]

On a deeper level, we can also recognise

D) an *axiological identity*, reflecting the deep values that govern the character's actions. Howard's original stories are based on a strong opposition *nature* vs. *culture*, represented through the theme *barbarism* vs. *civilisation*, where nature (and barbarism) are in the end regarded positively. These oppositions *nature* vs.

DOI: 10.1057/9781137434371.0006

culture also relate to other thematic categories such as *new* vs. *old, youth* vs. *old age, freedom* vs. *despotism, purity* vs. *corruption*, which were recurrent themes in America in the late nineteenth and early twentieth century and in much of Howard's work (Proietti, 2007; Bertetti, 2011). Another key theme in Howard's stories is *individuality* vs. *sociability*, or asserting one's individuality regarding social and cultural rules and conventions. Conan seems to pursue the path of absolute individual freedom (Tetro, 91), opposed to integration within a social body, whose values are recognised by the subject and are the horizon of his own fulfilment. In the following media expansions of Conan two main transformations can be observed: (1) the categories *nature* vs. *culture* and *barbarism* vs. *civilisation* remain, but the values attributed to them oscillate: in de Camp's stories civilisation, maturity and social integration, and responsibility are considered positively; (2) there are instances of re-categorisation, as in the case of the gradual transition, accomplished through Milius's film and the television series, from the thematic role of 'barbarian' to that of 'warrior'. This change subtends a replacement of the category barbarism vs. civilisation with the more normalised axiological category good vs. evil.

1.5   The Reboot of Conan

In the 1990s the fortune of Conan gradually declined. A project for a third film was shelved, and the live action and animated television series were unsuccessful. Between 1993 and 1995 all the comic book series gradually petered out, and in 1997 Tor Books stopped publishing pastiches. Moreover, hardcore fans were becoming increasingly dissatisfied with Conan Properties, owing to the company's lack of quality control and increasing disregard for Howard's original Conan stories (Sammons, 2007, 127–128).

Things started changing in 2002, when Paradox Entertainment, a Swedish video game producer, acquired Conan Properties Inc. The reboot of the character began with new philological editions of the original stories written by Howard (three hardback volumes published by Wandering Star and a paperback series published by Del Rey Books, 2003–2005). Different media platforms also added their contribution: in 2003, the first of five series by Dark Horse Comics came out; in 2008, the MMORPG (Massive Multiplayer Online Role-Playing Game) *Age of Conan: Hyborian Adventures* was released (one of many games); the film *Conan the Barbarian,* directed by Jason Momoa, appeared in 2011, and new series of *Age of Conan* books were published.

The rebuilding of the brand was based, at least initially, on two main-stays: firstly a greater adherence to Howard's original writings. This was done by following the Rippke timeline, as fans now considered de Camp's version obsolete and of little value. Secondly, a rigorous transmedial strategy would be pursued. Paradox Entertainment maintained strict control of the different media platforms so that every expansion would present different aspects of a shared and coherent universe. Sometimes they focused on parallel histories: in the *Age of Conan* MMORPG , Conan is not the main character; on the contrary, he does not intervene directly in the action, and only after having passed many levels does the player actually meet the Cimmerian, by now sitting on the throne of Aquilonia. The related novels even avoid showing Conan in person, instead, as with all the other products of the franchise, they introduce brand new char-acters and draw the receiver into a host of new adventures situated in the *Age of Conan*, exploiting the narrative potential offered by Howard's Hyborian Age.

Dark Horse Comics adopted a different strategy of narrative expan-sion. The ongoing series is unrelated to the Marvel's series. The stories tend to follow the Rippke timeline very closely and are based to a large degree on Howard's stories and material. Dark Horse's first two series were particularly praised by fans thanks to the fine scripts by Kurt Busiek and the wonderful illustrations by Cary North (later replaced by Tim Truman and Tomas Giorello). The first two series were indeed very close to the spirit and the stories by Howard. Initially published in episodes composed of six or seven issues, which were later bound in a single comic-book volume, the core story of each episode was an adapta-tion of a Howard story, expanded to include events that were implied in the original narrative. These were added before or tagged on to the end. In this sense, the series seemed to undergo a sort of *dilation* (Casetti, 1984, 10), or experience a form of 'hypertrophy in which each element is forced [...] to occupy time and space right to the end: an excess of presence of each cue' (Casetti, 1984, p. xx), with the result of delaying the end as long as possible.

This careful transmedial strategy was largely subverted in recent years. And this is particularly evident in Niespel's movie, *Conan the Barbarian.*

DOI: 10.1057/9781137434371.0006

After a troubled gestation period lasting over seven years, during which time actors, directors and even the production house changed repeatedly, the ill-fated film was eventually released in 2011. The result was mediocre and not very successful. Although the original intention was to create a Conan figure faithful to Howard's original, the cruel and idealistic character that emerged is in many ways a far cry from the original, abandoning any form of transmedia consistency. The first part is almost a remake of Milius's film, albeit with a different storyline, thus the two carefully studied criteria which were to determine the success of the reboot had fallen by the wayside.

To a certain extent this is also true of the most recent Dark Horse series, *Conan the Barbarian*, which features a creative re-interpretation of the Conan character far-removed from the original despite its adherence to the Rippke chronology. Furthermore, both the scripts by Brian Wood (depicting Conan in more human and realistic colours) and the illustrations (portraying a sort of controversial emo version of the traditional Conan) have attracted a lot of negative reactions from the more purist fans.

1.6   Conan the transmedial

In his ability to move across the different media, Conan the Barbarian is a good example of the character-centred logic that, in our opinion, is the basis of many older forms of transmedia expansions. Under this logic, which merges with the logic of transmedia storytelling, as intended by Jenkins (2006a), centred on the idea of a shared, fictional world, transmedial fictional coherency and consistency are less central. What is instead more important is the recognisability of the character and his identity, which must be ensured even if the character's features, in passing from one text to another and from one medium to another, are not always unequivocally defined.

Despite many of Conan's transmedia expansions across media coming relatively late in the character's history, his development in a single medium as a literary pulp hero clearly shows that some dynamics usually associated to with contemporary transmedia storytelling, such as the world-building and the production of user-generated content, were already operating in older storytelling practices – in particular, as we said in the introduction, in the aesthetics of the pulps. In the next chapter we will see how the narrative forms developed in pulp magazines emerged

DOI: 10.1057/9781137434371.0006

as a model for producing new strategies of transmedia storytelling in the late 1930s and 1940s.

Notes

1 Saying this I intend to exclude, in principle, mere adaptation or intersemiotic translations of a primary text. As Evans (2011, p. 27) states 'transmedia elements do not involve the telling of the same events on different platforms; they involve the telling of new events from the same storyworld'.

2 For more details on Howard's biography see Lord, 1976 and Finn, 2006.

3 A complete bibliography of all the Conan stories (originals and apocrypha) can be found in Gray and Precourt, 2005.

4 R. Howard, *The Phoenix on the Sword* (1932), in *The Coming of Conan the Cimmerian* (New York: Del Rey, 2003), p. 7.

5 Letter from R.E. Howard to P.S. Miller, 10 March 1936; published in http://www.barbariankeep.com/millerlet.html, date accessed 22 March 2014.

6 Revised and updated versions of the Miller-Clarke chronology appeared in 1986 (edited by Robert Jordan) and in 2000, by William Galen Gray. The latter includes all pastiches published in the 1980s, becoming an unlikely list of ongoing adventures.

7 The article titled 'Some Comments on Chronologies in Regards to the Conan Series' was published in two parts in the bulletin of the Robert E. Howard United Press Association, *REHupa* (#148 – December 1997 and #149 – February 1998).

8 Eco continues, '[This] does not change the psychological profile of the character, which has already been fixed, once and for all. [...] Instead of having characters put up with new adventures (that would imply their inexorable march toward death), they are made continually to relive their past. [...] Characters have a little future but an enormous past, and in any case, nothing of their past will ever have to change the mythological present in which they have been presented to the reader from the beginning' (1985, pp. 168–169).

9 The novelisation of John Milius's movie *Conan the Barbarian* should be added here, written by de Camp and Carter. Closely connected to this series are two short stories by A.J. Offutt (*Conan and the Sorcerer*, 1978, and *Conan the Mercenary*, 1981) published by Ace Books in a paperback collection and illustrated by Esteban Maroto.

10 Other Marvel Conan titles were published over the years in *Savage Tales* and other ephemeral series. Moreover a newspaper comic strip appeared daily from 4 September 1978 to 12 April 1981. It was originally written by Roy Thomas and illustrated by John Buscema and Ernie Chan.

DOI: 10.1057/9781137434371.0006

11   A complete overview should also include computer games, role-playing games, action figures, cards, a MMORPG and other media forms. For more details, see Sammon 2007 and Bertetti 2011.

12   See Greimas and Courtés, 1979.

13   This is the description of the Cimmerian that Howard makes at the beginning of 'The Slithering Shadows': 'He stood like a bronze image in the sand, apparently impervious to the murderous sun, though his only garment was a silk loin-cloth, girdled by a wide gold-buckled belt from which hung a saber and a broad-bladed poniard. On his clean-cut limbs were evidences of scarcely healed wounds ... [His] blue eyes [were] smoldering savagely from under his black tousled mane, as if the desert were a tangible enemy'. R. Howard, 'The Slithering Shadows' (1933), in *The Conan Chronicles. Volume 1: The People of the Black Circle* (London: Gollancz, 2003), p. 443.

14   In 'The Queen of the Black Coast' Conan says, 'Let me live deep while I live; let me know the rich juices of red meat and stinging wine on my palate, the hot embrace of white arms, the mad exultation of battle when the blue blades flame and crimson, and I am content [...] I live, I burn with life, I love, I slay and am content'. R. Howard, 'The Queen of the Black Coast' (1934), in *The Conan Chronicles,* p. 127.

15   However, note that the prophecy was invented by Roy Thomas in the first episode of Marvel's *Conan the Barbarian* series, not by TV series writers; it also appears in Milius's movie. However in both cases its impact on Conan's motivation to acting is quite limited. See Bertetti 2011 for further details.

DOI: 10.1057/9781137434371.0006

2

Superman: Building a Transmedia World for a Comic Book Hero

Matthew Freeman

Abstract: *This chapter aims to explore the transmedia fiction of Superman from a storyworld-centered approach. Exploring transmedia storytelling during the early- to mid-twentieth-century America, I examine how attributes of pulp fiction – its narrative structures, its production style, and its effect on audienceengagement – developed an alignment between pulp magazines, comic books and strips, radio dramas and movie serials during the 1930s and 1940s. Specifically, and by using Superman and his storyworld as a case study, the chapter considers how this alignment encouraged connections between media that facilitated transmedia storytelling.*

Keywords: narrative expansion; pulp fiction; seriality; Superman; transmedia storytelling; world-building

Scolari, Carlos A., Paolo Bertetti, and Matthew Freeman. *Transmedia Archaeology: Storytelling in the Borderlines of Science Fiction, Comics and Pulp Magazines.* Basingstoke: Palgrave Macmillan, 2014. DOI: 10.1057/9781137434371.0007.

2.1   From barbarians to superheroes

While transmedia scholarship is peppered with occasional historical asides and consideration (Jenkins, 2014; Johnson, 2013; Santo, 2010) – and indeed other research is beginning to emerge on the subject of historical transmedia (Freeman, 2014a; Freeman, 2014b; Scolari, 2014) – the value of this discussion can be enriched if considered from other analytical and methodological categories. If transmedia storytelling, as reiterated in the Introduction to this book, is characterised broadly by the expansion of narrative through different media forms as well as the production of user-generated content, then through which creative processes and cultural backdrops may such characteristics develop? We propose that transmedia may come to operate from a whole plethora of influences – some historical, some contemporary. Deciphering at least some of those influences is the aim of this book.

We have come to understand the prominent influence that convergence and participatory culture plays on these developments in a contemporary setting (Jenkins, 2006a). New forms of digital technology have brought with them new forms of technological convergence that allows audiences to engage more actively in media content and fictional storyworlds (Meikle and Young, 2012). But in exploring the potentially different creative processes and cultural backdrops that have encouraged a narrative to expand through media – by tracing and uncovering the various archaeologies of transmedia storytelling – we can begin to fully understand why transmedia storytelling operates in the way that it does.

Achieving this end means employing different methodological approaches that reconcile the past with the present; looking for historical precedents of transmedia must mean searching in different places while simultaneously tracing the historical and contemporary through-lines. Given how common it has become to theorise transmedia storytelling as part of the structures and organisational systems of the corporately converged and integrated media conglomerate, we can propose that transmedia is itself contingent upon the alignment of multiple fields of media production. Without such alignments, wherever they may fall, it is doubtful whether a narrative can flow across multiple media in the fluent, coherent way that seems a prerequisite to transmedia storytelling. Yet these alignments can, and indeed have, changed over time. 'Media are not stable entities,' writes Anthony Smith, 'but rather protean cultural formations, each with elements that can vary greatly, including the capacity of technologies, the composition of audiences, the organisation of regional markets and the economic strategies of media institutions' (2012, 5). Media industries are delineated by changing and ever-shifting conditions. As these industrial conditions align and realign over time, the methods actually underpinning how a transmedia narrative is produced must similarly realign and reconfigure.

This chapter expands the book's archaeological exploration of transmedia storytelling by exploring how this phenomenon operated during the late 1930s and early 1940s in America. Having defined the corpus of our 'transmedia pulp fiction' in the book's Introduction, this chapter works to examine how attributes of pulp fiction – its narrative structures, its production style and its effect on how many audiences engaged with its stories – developed a common alignment between certain types of media formats. This alignment will reveal key strategies of transmedia storytelling – specifically narrative expansions – during the 1930s and 1940s. We examine the ways in which the forms of pulp magazines, comic books/strips, radio dramas and cinema – specifically movie serials – each came to actively cross-pollinate one another during this period, encouraging dialogues and connections that were useful for developing common tendencies towards transmedia storytelling at that particular time.

Hence by using Superman and the character's fictional storyworld as a case study, we demonstrate how the dynamics of this cross-pollination facilitated the construction of a coherent transmedial storyworld for Superman. We begin by examining the influence of earlier defined narrative attributes of pulp fiction on early Superman comics in the late 1930s, helping to form these comics as an expansive storyworld, built across multiple comic books and newspaper strips. I also touch upon the utilisation of active audience participation at this time, a key component of transmedia today, on the continuing transmedial development of Superman in the early 1940s by exploring the character's popular Superman Day. Subsequently, the chapter moves on to explore how the same pulp narrative strategies specified earlier – those being narrative implication and expansion, seriality and retroactive linkages – manifested in the media of radio and cinema, hence revealing how pulp-orientated narratology enabled the Superman storyworld to be built and expand across media as an exemplar of historical transmedia storytelling.

DOI: 10.1057/9781137434371.0007

2.2   Stepping stones of entertainment

On the level of basic narrative, at least, we have seen in the Introduction to this book how current definitions of transmedia storytelling are in some ways underpinned by certain attributes of storytelling that cut across historical and contemporary media alike, albeit working differently in different eras. These attributes comprise, firstly, seriality, secondly, what Gregory Steirer calls narrative expansion and implication, and finally what Mark J. P. Wolf terms retroactive linkages. Each of these concepts served as strategies for expanding a fictional world in the media of the past – such as, prominently, pulp magazines. Of course, while none of these strategies was exclusive to pulp fiction, the examples cited earlier in the book's Introduction do serve to demonstrate the role of pulp narratology on approaches to expanding a fictional world across borders. This combination of attributes would lead to a certain style of storytelling and audience engagement that is important for understanding transmedia storytelling as a historical phenomenon during the twentieth century.

To quickly recap these particular attributes, narrative implication, according to Steirer, sees 'the details of a single, self-contained story gestur[ing] to additional histories, events, characters, or locations not fully developed within the story itself' (2011). Narrative implication thus implies the existence of untold stories, hinting at a larger storyworld beyond the confines of the narrative taking place – a further series of spaces where concurrent adventures are unfolding. Relatedly, narrative expansion 'involves the expansion of a given narrative beyond the confines of a single text, usually in such a way that many of the original characters, settings, and histories are preserved and/or further developed through encounters with new characters, settings, and events' (Steirer, 2011).

In transmedia storytelling, seriality henceforth emerges as a key component for extending narrative across borders, a conception that Edgar Rice Burroughs also hinted towards in our Introduction when he recognised how pulp storytelling may work like a series of stepping stones, each stone an event that leads to the next chapter – the leap between stones a metaphor for keeping readers hooked on what will happen next. Indeed, a final narratological aspects intrinsic to the phenomenon of transmedia storytelling identified earlier, and one further hinted at by Burroughs in relation to a very different context, is the notion of world-building, 'the process of designing a fictional

DOI: 10.1057/9781137434371.0007

universe that [...] is sufficiently detailed to enable many different stories to emerge but coherent so that each story feels like it fits with the others' (Jenkins, 2006a, 335). We specifically wish to pick up on these four narratological attributes in this chapter, examining the influence of these pulp conceptions on how comic books, radio and cinema served to expand stories across media. In leading us to see where transmedia storytelling may have evolved from and from which configurations, this approach will provide for a clearer grasp of transmedia storytelling as a trans-historical practice of media production.

2.3   Through the valley of *The Shadow*

The most prominent cross-industrial pollination of the pulp form was in fact on the emerging medium of comic books, which arrived in the 1930s as the heirs to the pulp tradition. Paul Lopes argues that comic books were formed as 'a product of recombinant culture: a new hybrid born from pulp fiction and comic art' (2009, 46). Comic books exploited similar techniques of seriality, narrative implication, expansion and retroactive linkages in the aim of building a storyworld. With their ongoing narrative deferral, the serialised, world-building format of pulp magazines provided a blueprint for ways to reduce the financial risk in comic strip and indeed comic book publishing, with the pulp's success at both seriality with characters crossing back and forth across different iterations stemming from its 'capacity to nurture the type of loyal consumer that purchases and engages with a succession of narrative instalments so as to discover "what happened next"' (Hagedorn, 1988, 12).

William H. Young Jr., for instance, defines the period's adventure comic books as that which 'work[ed] with a day-to-day serial plot, usually devoid of humour, and filled with physical action', noting that the form 'grew out of the serial tradition [...] and borrowed more freely from other media than any previous comic form' (1969, 405–406). Pulp genres such as adventure migrated to the comic book page in the 1930s. Examples included the crime strip, as epitomised by *The Shadow*, which debuted in comic strip form on 17 June 1931, and the science fiction strip, with *Buck Rogers* – once a pulp story first published in *Amazing Stories* magazine in August 1928 – similarly migrating to the newspaper comic strip shortly thereafter. This brought the arrival of the comic book, as many pulp artists, illustrators and publishers crossed over into comic

DOI: 10.1057/9781137434371.0007

book publishing. As David Saunders writes, '[t]he comics as we know them are rooted in that late great period of American writing known as Pulp Fiction ... For one thing, many of the artists and illustrators crossed over from the pulps to the comics' (2012).One notable example was Harry Donenfeld, a prolific pulp fiction publisher in the 1920s who became enormously significant to the birth of Superman.

According to a report published in *The Film Daily* in 1942, the birth of Superman began with 'a chap named Harry Donenfeld, a prosperous printer, publisher and distributor of "pulp" magazines.' 'It was on [Donenfeld's] desk that the comic strip character was really born,' continued *The Washington Post*. 'He was the first man to recognize the appeal of the mighty man when two shy boys from Cleveland, Jerry Siegel and Joe Shuster, introduced Superman to him' (22 October 1940, 19). Much like a typical pulp, *Action Comics* #1 – featuring the debut appearance of Superman – was an anthology, a collection of 11 adventure stories. *Action Comics* #1 was published in June 1938; its publisher, DC Comics, triggered a superhero boom. Superman would materialise from an accumulation of pulp narrative strategies detailed earlier, building the fiction as a storyworld that extended across multiple media in the same way as the earlier pulps had extended across multiple editions.

Through examining the ways in which *Action Comics* #1 incorporated narrative strategies of narrative implication and expansion, particularly – both borrowed in this instance from earlier pulp-based characteristics – we can see how the Superman storyworld was constructed as a space ripe for transmedial development. In terms of the core plot featured inside *Action Comics* #1, the comic revealed that Superman is the last survivor of an unknown distant planet, sent to Earth in a spaceship as an infant seconds before the far-off planet's destruction. Found by two passing motorists, called the Kents, and raised as a journalist called Clark Kent, readers were informed that Superman possesses remarkable physical strength and fights a never-ending battle for truth and justice, all the while disguised as a reporter working for the *Daily Planet*.

Beyond this *Action Comics* #1 used strategies that might be understood in terms of narrative implication – strategies underpinning our comprehension of transmedia storytelling. Firstly, for instance, we should consider genre. Even today, fantasy and science fiction seem crucial for techniques of transmedia storytelling, with notable contemporary examples such as *The Matrix*, *Star Wars*, *Doctor Who*, *Lost* and

DOI: 10.1057/9781137434371.0007

Heroes all operating within these genres. The nature of world-creating in these genres is much more evident than in crime or mystery stories, for example, or even horror stories. Writing that 'the rapt upward gaze of faces bathed in light in Steven Spielberg's *Close Encounters of the Third Kind* (1977) is emblematic of the expansive thrust of science fiction,' Barry Keith Grant argues that 'vision in [...] science fiction gazes up and out – from one man's small steps in Jules Verne's *From the Earth to the Moon* (1865) to the giant step for mankind through the stargate in Stanley Kubrick's *2001: A Space Odyssey* (1968)' (2004, 17). Science fiction often explores possible or parallel worlds, building open fictional spaces that promote a 'sense of wonder' (Redmond, 2004, 3).

This notion of an open, outward-looking storyworld is important for understanding one of the ways through which storyworlds are constructed transmedially. We can argue that fantasy stories such as Tarzan, science-fictional superhero tales such as Superman and contemporary instances of the genre such as *The Matrix* all construct parallel storyworlds. In *Tarzan of the Apes*, it is between the civilisation and the jungle; in *The Matrix*, the parallel divides are between the real world and the artificial dream world. In Superman, too, we can highlight the parallel between the other world of Superman's alien home and the world of Earth where Superman now resides.

This creation of other, parallel worlds within the sphere of the larger fictional storyworld can be understood as a further example of what Steirer has termed narrative implication. By acknowledging the existence of a parallel story space – one where other stories have once happened or are now happening – science fiction can construct 'a single, self-contained story [that] gestures to additional histories, events, characters, or locations not fully developed within the story itself' (Steirer, 2011).

For example, in *Action Comics* #1 readers were shown an alien planet moments before it exploded. However, they did not know what this planet was, where it existed in the universe, what its name was, or why it even exploded. Immediately there was a sense of mystery surrounding this planet, its writers gesturing to the possibility of untold tales about the planet. This style was reflective of much of what had come to be understood as pulp fiction – the serial sagas of science fiction and adventure heroes featuring lost worlds that scattered pieces of a character's or world's mythology across countless editions, in turn emphasising gaps in the larger story that could only be bridged by the reader's continued consumption.

DOI: 10.1057/9781137434371.0007

This gap in the mysterious history of Superman's home planet was to be scattered far outside the terrain of comic books – expanded across into the character's newspaper comic strip. The *Superman* newspaper comic strip, first published in January 1939, took the Superman origin story narrated in *Action Comics* #1 and expanded this origin story, providing readers with more story information about the mythology of the storyworld. In other words, it exploited strategies of narrative expansion – expanding 'a given narrative beyond the confines of a single text, usually in such a way that many of the original characters, settings, and histories are preserved and/or further developed through encounters with new characters, settings, and events' (Steirer, 2011. In the *Superman* newspaper strip, for example, the initially unknown and mysterious alien planet was given a name, Krypton. Readers were presented with new information concerning the events behind its earlier destruction along with a more scientific explanation for Superman's strength.

Names were also given to Superman's parents, Jor-El and Lora, with the Kryptonian name of the hero revealed to be Kal-El. Such an emphasis on narrative expansion across textual borders mirrored Burroughs' *At the Earth's Core*, a pulp story that situated its own narrative events in the backstory of *Tarzan and the Jewels of Opar* so as to merge two distinct fictions – and indeed two potentially different readerships – into one. Yet this strategy also echoes that of contemporary discussions of transmedia storytelling. Jenkins, for instance, observed how transmedia storytelling has come to mean additional texts that 'draw on backstory' (2006a, 96), 'each step along the way buil[ding] on what has come before' (2006a, 97). In much the same way that Burroughs' pulps cited in the Introduction presented a retroactively linked fictional world where the stories of one title provided geographical context to the stories of another, serialised and interwoven across multiple editions, the comics of Superman had similarly established themselves as part of a serialised, retroactively linked fictional universe where the Superman adventures existed in the same realm as other heroes, such as Batman.

Batman was a pulp-inspired crime-fighting vigilante created by Bob Kane and Bill Finger, first appearing in *Detective Comics* #27 in May 1939. Pairing the two popular characters was a logical business move, and in 1940, only one year after his debut, Batman shared the cover with Superman for the 1940 *New York World's Fair* comic. Having Superman and Batman on the same comic issue, sharing the front cover in ways signalling their sharing of the same storyworld, was a narratological

DOI: 10.1057/9781137434371.0007

tactic of world-building that had once defined the retroactive linkages of the pulps. Moreover, in borrowing the narrative arsenal from the pulps, embracing pulpification in ways that tied new story spaces as serialised extensions of a larger storyworld where characters from one story appeared in another, DC Comics came to exploit a number of narrative attributes that would ultimately define the aesthetic of transmedia storytelling. Comic strips/books are in this sense central to the evolution of transmedia storytelling. This medium, evolving as it did from pulp fiction, became a prime example of seriality in the days before television. Important narratological attributes of implication and expansion, of world-building, became embedded into the creative fabric of comic book stories. Their inheritance of pulp genres such as fantasy and science fiction was indeed crucial to this world-creation process.

2.4   Out to space

The *New York World's Fair* comic book was in fact not available to purchase at newsstands in the same way as ordinary comic books of the period. Instead, this particular comic book was only available at *The World's Fair* on 3 July 1940 – aka Superman Day. This event saw the first public appearance of Superman, extending the character once again. Superman Day was in many respects an embodiment of the narrative scatter that had delineated pulp-fiction narratology. 'From 9 o'clock in the morning,' reported *The New York Times*, 'registration [opened] for the contest to determine America's Super-Boy and Super-Girl' (3 July 1940, 14). Superman Day featured Superman in full costume, parading in front of a crowd before performing a scripted adventure for the audience. The event was predominantly promotional for the sale of the *New York World's Fair* comic book, a special edition. Alongside the above contest and sales tables for the comic, Superman Day included 'a band [that] paraded about town giving concerts before Superman performances and the stage setting of the performance in turn served as the setting for the [comic's] prologue' (*The Film Daily*, 3 July 1940, 180).

Superman Day had created an interactive media experience for Superman, with the fictional world of the story permeating outside of the physical space of comic books and into the streets. Audiences began to interact with Superman, migrating from comic books to the event in

DOI: 10.1057/9781137434371.0007

ways that echo Jenkins' characterisation of contemporary transmedia audiences. For Jenkins, the process of 'creating transmedia storyworlds' is itself the process of 'understanding how to appeal to migratory audiences' (2008). Superman Day represented an integrated transmedia experience – the fictional adventure of the *New York World's Fair* comic combined with the spectatorial spaces of the day in ways that created an integrated, cross-pollinated transmedia attraction. Further, *The World's Fair* event was also broadcast live on *The Adventures of Superman* radio serial, providing a further point of cross-pollinated, transmedial connection.

Texts such as *Action Comics* #1, the *Superman* newspaper comic strip, and indeed events such as Superman Day began the process of transforming Superman stories into an anthology of expansive, world-building narratives. Bridging alternate media forms of the period, the Superman adventures were fast becoming a world-building pulp patchwork of transmedial narratives. Much has been said in this chapter already about the ways in which the inherent narratological form of pulp magazines and their serial fragmentation of an expanding, often adjoining storyworld – each chapter broken up into segments and scattered across several issues – itself served as a narratological blueprint for the dissemination of Superman texts across multiple media. In fact, a complex cross-pollination between pulp magazines, radio dramas, and, particularly, movie serials was steadily intensifying throughout the twentieth century. Similar pulp-based storytelling devices and genre categories began to pulpify generic categories on radio, as these devices came to define how the medium produced its content.

For instance, Alexander Russo notes how the start of the 1940s witnessed a great increase in the number of adventure thrillers being produced, 'reflecting the popularity of the mystery, detective, and crime pulp fiction' (2002, 185). Central to these genres was a similar emphasis on seriality and, in turn, world-building as well as the gradual, expansive linkages of multiple iterations of a storyworld. The practice of serialising a story first in and, later, across media became the backbone of transcribed radio dramas in the 1930s and 1940s – a period that saw a dominant transition from live to recorded programming. The wide adoption of seriality that is recognised in this chapter as a cornerstone of transmedia storytelling occurred, as Smith has reinforced, 'precisely due to the emergence of industrialised production' (2012, 8).

The Adventures of Superman radio serial was first broadcast by Mutual Broadcasting System on 12 February 1940. Much of the radio programming aimed at children during this time often took the form of the serial or the adventure cliffhanger, a format designed to keep its child listeners coming back every night in much the same way as pulp magazines had worked previously. Examples of these adventure cliffhangers included pulp thrillers such as *The Shadow*, *Buck Rogers*, *The Green Hornet* and *The Lone Ranger*. *The Adventures of Superman* broadcast alongside such similarly pulp-orientated adventure serials. As Ford suggested of the process of transmedial world-building earlier, these programmes made use of a serialised storytelling structure, multiple creative forces which author various parts of the story, a sense of long-term continuity, a deep character backlog, and therein a sense of permanence.

This deep character backlog saw new additions to the Superman story-world, with multiple creative forces authoring various parts of the story. Narrative expansion came into play when Jimmy Olsen, a photographer working at the *Daily Planet*, was introduced inside *Action Comics* #6 in November 1938 before appearing on radio in expanded form. In April 1940, *The Adventures of Superman* introduced Jimmy Olsen to Clark Kent, unveiling new story information such as how Jimmy began working at the *Daily Planet*. In this way, the radio programme continued the pulps' earlier tendency to scatter story content across texts, echoing Steirer's narrative implication strategy, alluding to 'distinctive characters with incomplete backstories' – itself an important characteristic of transmedia storytelling (Jenkins, 2006a, 96).

Similarly, *The Adventures of Superman* radio serial compounded the aforementioned attempt to link the storyworld of Superman with the storyworld of Batman. In March 1945, Superman and Batman appeared on radio together for the first time. It was the first of many regular appearances for Batman on *The Adventures of Superman*, a strategy devised partly from the rising popularity of Superman and the radio's heavy thrice-weekly production schedules. There were no reruns in the 1940s; Superman needed to appear on air three times a week regardless of any writer fallouts or staff shortages. On many occasions Batman and Robin appeared on radio in Superman's absence, filling in for the Man of Steel when Superman voice actor Bud Collyer fell ill. Despite the production-based practicalities motivating many of these appearances, then, we should not overlook the fact that the (re)appearance of Batman on *The Adventures of Superman* radio serial constituted a further instance of transmedia storytelling. Echoing Wolf's conception of the retroactive linkage – a joining of two independently created fictional worlds

DOI: 10.1057/9781137434371.0007

that previously had existed separately, usually through a character that appears in both worlds (2012, 380–381) – Superman had continued to flow and expand across multiple media forms, a transmedial development also true of the cinema.

2.5   Across the universe

Indeed, the year 1913 has seen the birth of the American movie serial – a form of cinema that made extensive use of narrative expansion, typically framed around adventure and science fiction genres. Movie serials comprised a succession of films with a continuous story, usually screened over the course of a number of weeks or months. The movie serial first began when motion picture producers and magazine editors or publishers started to collaborate with one another, working together to tell a story across magazines and films simultaneously. If the pulps, comics and radio could exploit a crossover correlation, then why couldn't the cinema do the same?

The first instance of this is widely believed to have been Thomas Edison's *What Happened to Mary?*, released in collaboration with *The Ladies' World* publication in 1913, wherein select instalments of the story appeared 'in print just before the theatrical exhibition of each episode' (Singer, 1990, 170). As Karlton C. Lahue asserts, 'the practice of linking films with serial publication in magazines was the essential ingredient leading to the great success of the [movie] serial' (1964, 7). By 1914, many of the silent movie serial producers had discovered that they could generate interest in their serials by 'teasing the audience' (Lahue, 1964, 7).

Of course, this strategy had also worked well for the mystery of *The Shadow*'s secret identity, which was similarly scattered across multiple editions of pulp magazines. Movie serials such as *Million Dollar Mystery* in 1914 even exploited the interactive participation of the audience, a tactic that had worked particularly well for consumer magazines in ways that saw the producers of the film offering a $10,000 prize to the viewer who submitted 'an original and clever ending' (*Moving Picture World* 9 February 1914). The movie serial had in this way developed practices based partly on similar narratological strategies from the pulps; both forms effectively strove to increase the drawing power of a story and increase audience engagement with the text via seriality and narrative expansion. Among these strategies was the serial cliffhanger, the practice

DOI: 10.1057/9781137434371.0007

of leaving the story unfinished to entice audiences back. Yet where the pulps would exploit strategies of seriality and narrative implication and expansion in the same medium, the movie serial, in mimicking the formulas and structures of this period's pulps, built upon this fragmentary storytelling apparatus, developing such strategies into apparatus that could also extend across media.

Accordingly, a number of successful movie serials based on comic strip characters flooded the cinema throughout the first half of the twentieth century. Movie serials, Jason Scott notes, 'became much more closely associated with pre-existing characters in the Sunday comics' – and, in later decades, with comic books and radio serials (2009). *Superman* (1948) and *Atom Man vs. Superman* (1950), for example, two movie serials based on the DC Comics character, exemplify this trend. By the late 1940s, as Gary Grossman writes, Hollywood commonly exploited 'the audiences' support for their daily print favourites [by] constructing film adventures around them' (1977, 17). In January 1948, *Variety* reported that Columbia Pictures would be producing a movie serial based on 'the comic strip and radio serial Superman [...] filmed as a 15-chapter cliff-hanger' (9 January 1948, 3). Columbia had by this time developed a reputation for specialising in movie serials based on comic book/ pulp heroes. Prominent examples included *The Shadow* in 1940 and *The Phantom* and *Batman* in 1943 – all of which came in the aftermath of the superhero boom spawned by Superman.

From a production and audience standpoint, the American movie serials in the 1940s shared notable overlaps with the pulps, a correlation and cross-pollination that would enable certain transmedial crossovers between these media to intensify. Movie serials were principally B-movies, deemed cheap and trashy like the pulps had been. At this time, Tino Balio writes, 'many of the B films were directed toward specific theatres, audience groups, and classes of spectators. Such genres as B Westerns were, like serials, aimed at a quick payoff in minor houses attracting the Saturday matinee and juvenile audiences' (1995, 326). Balio further observes that 'the narrative traits of [movie serials] echoed the pulps [...] Serials have similar action-orientated heroes, displaying fisticuffs, athleticism, and cheery youthfulness. [Serials] move rapidly, loading the narrative with action-filled incidents' (1995, 334). Comic books had of course derived from pulp fiction – and Superman creators Jerry Siegel and Joe Shuster both worked for a pulp magazine before joining DC Comics. The cinema outlet that was chosen to house Superman

DOI: 10.1057/9781137434371.0007

in the late 1940s period was thus similarly associated with the pulps. Narratively, at least, movie serials placed the same emphasis on 'simple, standardised, and repetitive plots' (Balio 1995, 333).

Exploiting further transmedia-associated strategies of seriality and narrative expansion, then, 1948's *Superman* and its sequel *Atom Man vs. Superman* operated as transmedial extensions of the Superman comics and, in particular, the radio serial. The serialised narratives of the latter began to flow across into the adventures of the movie serials. For example, in *Atom Man vs. Superman*, the alter-ego of Atom Man was revealed to be Lex Luthor, Superman's arch-nemesis since 1940. *Atom Man vs. Superman* had extended the narrative of the radio serial; what may have seemed like two distinct iterations of Superman – and thus two distinct storyworlds – were retroactively linked. For those who consumed these various Superman texts across different media, the adventures of Superman had again grown into pulp-inflected stepping stones of entertainment. In effect, *Atom Man vs. Superman* narrated the story taking place after a select episode broadcast on radio. Audiences were hereby provided with a depth of story knowledge – the movie serial exploiting seriality and narrative expansion to promote an audience's consumption of an expansive storyworld that unfolded across multiple media.

In addition, earlier explored pulp strategies such as Wolf's conception of the retroactive linkage – joining two distinct storyworld as part of a single, larger fictional universe where characters cross over – continued to play a major role in the process of building the Superman world across media. One plot point in the aforementioned *Atom Man vs. Superman* movie serial saw Lex Luthor trap Superman in another dimension. This dimension, named here The Empty Doom, was represented as a limbo-like prison-world – a space that would later be renamed The Phantom Zone and become a longstanding staple of the Superman storyworld. The Phantom Zone would eventually appear in *Superman* #158 in January 1963, but as a story space it had already been created by author Edmond Hamilton in the Captain Future novel *Planets in Peril* in 1942 – a fictional world far outside of the universe of Superman, or so it seemed. Captain Future was a science-fictional pulp hero in the vein of Conan – a space-travelling scientist turned adventurer – originally published as a pulp magazine throughout the 1940s. Hamilton later went on to write some of the early Superman stories for DC Comics, including some of the earliest comic-book appearances of The Phantom Zone. In 1954, The Phantom Zone would also be used as the arsenal to bridge the world of Superman

DOI: 10.1057/9781137434371.0007

with the world of Wonder Woman, when in *Wonder Woman* #70 the titular heroine was banished to The Phantom Zone on her wedding day. If the pulps were significant in the way that they used storytelling to build storyworlds across texts, once again we can understand why comic books continued many of these same storytelling strategies – encouraging the narratives of these genres to extend and unite across other media in cinema and radio.

2.6   A world of adventure

Adventure, mystery, science fiction and fantasy – from these pulp genres would spring new storytelling outlets: pulp magazines, radio dramas, adventure comic strips and movie serials. Each of these media forms began to acquire and share particular narrative attributes during this period that, while initially characteristic of the pulp form, had in turn become staples of the flourishing cross-industrial practice of transmedia storytelling once the pulp heroes of these magazines began to reappear across the divides of multiple media. In assessing the ways in which the adventures of Superman – 'a progenitor in the pop folklore of the twentieth century' (Arnold, 1978, 11) – were adopted and expanded across the media forms of comic books and newspaper strips, special events, radio dramas and finally the cinema, this chapter has demonstrated how many of the narrative characteristics of past pulp magazines were also adopted and expanded across and infused upon these other media forms.

This infusion fortified a cross-pollination of narrative practices between these media in ways that allowed for particular narratological arsenal of these once culturally marginalised pulp fictions to become increasingly industrialised historical practices of transmedia storytelling in and across the period's larger, mass entertainment industries. As noted in the previous chapter, a fictional world is not only a state of things or a common setting, but also a combination of transformations acted within that world. Aaron Clayton reinforces this general significance, pointing to the role of crossover characters specifically – itself an extension of the retroactive linkages associated with both historical pulp fictions and contemporary transmedia fictions. Clayton observes how this characteristic developed in later comic books, providing *Tarzan vs. Predator: At Earth's Core* and *Batman/Tarzan: Claws of the Cat-Woman*, published in 1997 and 2000 respectively, as examples (2012, 181).

DOI: 10.1057/9781137434371.0007

If transmedia storytelling is itself 'a process where integral elements of a fiction get dispersed systematically across multiple [media] channels for the purpose of creating a unified and coordinated entertainment experience' (Jenkins, 2011), then following this logic we have seen how the practice shares clear and important narratological similarities with the structure of the historical pulp magazine. Both pulps and transmedia storytelling are about re-forming – most typically via seriality, narrative implication, narrative expansion and retroactive world-building linkages – a series of distinct or anthological narratives into one grand mythology, chopped and shuffled into interactive entertainment stepping stones across multiple media.

DOI: 10.1057/9781137434371.0007

3

El Eternauta: Transmedia Expansions, Political Resistance and Popular Appropriations of a Human Hero

Carlos A. Scolari

▶

Abstract: *This chapter describes the origins of* El Eternauta *– one of the most powerful science fiction stories ever told – and its successive expansions to other media. After a description of this fictional world, the chapter analyses the political appropriations of this comic – originally created by Héctor Germán Oesterheld and Francisco Solano López – by young political movements in contemporary Argentina. The case of* El Eternauta *– a character born in the late 1950s – confirms that transmedia storytelling is not just a commercial phenomenon: it goes beyond the media business and opens new dimensions to political activism.*

Keywords: alien invasion; Argentina; comic; *El Eternauta*; Nestornauta; Oesterheld; science fiction

Scolari, Carlos A., Paolo Bertetti, and Matthew Freeman. *Transmedia Archaeology: Storytelling in the Borderlines of Science Fiction, Comics and Pulp Magazines*. Basingstoke: Palgrave Macmillan, 2014. DOI: 10.1057/9781137434371.0008.

3.1   *El Eternauta*: Brief story of a classic

This chapter starts with a strong affirmation: *El Eternauta* should be considered both the greatest Argentine science fiction story and the most significant Argentine comic. To understand *El Eternauta*'s privileged position in the cultural production of Argentine society, it is necessary to map the territory of the popular genres and mass culture in the Argentina of the 1950s.

The 1950s were the golden age of Argentine comics. A large number of foreign artists arrived to the country after the war ended in Europe. There were many important Italian comic-book artists living in Argentina at that time; artists like Mario Faustinelli, Hugo Pratt, Ivo Pavone and Dino Battaglia were known as the Venice Group. Alberto Breccia and Francisco Solano López – two graphic artists from Uruguay and Paraguay respectively – and Héctor Germán Oesterheld – an Argentine writer – joined the group and worked together with the Europeans. In the 1950s, high-circulation magazines with comic strips arrived to the newsstands: *Rico Tipo* (1944), *Intervalo* (1945), *Patoruzito* (1945) and *Misterix* (1948). Although it included several Italian comics, *Misterix* had its own production and played a central role in the Argentine comic panorama.

In 1956, Oesterheld and his brother Jorge created a new publishing house – Editorial Frontera – and two new magazines: *Frontera* (1957) and *Hora Cero* (1957). The experience was so successful that in the following years new satellite publications joined the newsstands: *Hora Cero Semanal*, *Hora Cero Extra* and *Frontera Extra*. Many of the most important characters of Argentine comics were published in these magazines: *Sargento Kirk* (Oesterheld-Pratt), *Ernie Pike* (Oesterheld-Pratt), *Ticonderoga* (Oesterheld-Pratt), *Randall the Killer* (Oesterheld-del Castillo), *Sherlock Time* (Oesterheld-Breccia), *Joe Zonda* (Oesterheld-López), *Verdugo Ranch* (Oesterheld-Pavone), *Leonero Brent* (Oesterheld–Moliterni) and *Rolo, el marcianoadoptivo* (Oesterheld-López). As will be seen, Oesterheld was the main writer behind these narratives (sometimes under the name of H. Sturgiss or C. de la Vega). Many of these characters arrived to Europe in the next decade, when artists like Hugo Pratt went back to their countries. In July 1967, the Italian publisher Florenzo Ivaldi launched *Sgt. Kirk,* a new comic magazine inspired by Oesterheld's character. It started publishing *Unaballatadel mare salato* in the following months, the first story of the *Corto Maltese* saga by Hugo Pratt.

DOI: 10.1057/9781137434371.0008

But let us go back to Editorial Frontera. On 4 September 1957, a new comic called *El Eternauta* written by Oesterheld and illustrated by Solano López came out in *Hora Cero Semanal* (Oesterheld and López, 1975). The first version of the comic, which would transform Argentine graphics and science fiction narrative, lasted until 1959. It was a successful product that consolidated the position of the publishing house in the Argentine market (Ferreira, 2010, 2012; Sasturain, 1982, 1995, 2012; Scolari, 1998).

Before analyzing *El Eternauta* we can reflect on the philosophy behind Frontera's works: What characterised these productions? Oesterheld introduced a new perspective in the comic narrative: we could say that the 'comic for adults' was born in Argentina in the 1950s. A new approach based on controverting the stereotypes of traditional comics – for example, negating the role of the hero – was at the centre of these stories. Oesterheld opened a new path to comic storytelling in a very similar way to the narrative revolution led by artists like Alan Moore (*Watchmen*, 1986–1987) and Frank Miller (*Batman: The Dark Knight Returns*, 1986) in the 1980s (Coma, 1984; Scolari, 1998).

However, the golden age of Argentine comics would not last for long. The arrival of foreign publications from Mexico started a financial crisis in the Argentine comic industry, and several publishers, including Oesterheld's Ediciones Frontera, had to close down or be sold, which forced several artists and writers to go abroad. Oesterheld sold his publishing house to Editorial Emilio Ramírez, who reissued *El Eternauta* in a dedicated magazine in 1961. But the golden age was almost over. Between 1962 and 1964, Oesterheld and Alberto Breccia created *Mort Cinder,* which may be the culminant moment but at the same time final point of the Argentine comic golden age.[1]

3.1.1   *El Eternauta* (1957–1959)

El Eternauta is a story of survival. A group of citizens (Juan Salvo, his family and a heterogeneous company of people from different professions and social classes) must survive an alien invasion. The invasion starts with a deadly phosphorescent snowfall and continues with the arrival of a series of alien species that apply high-level technologies. If H.G. Wells bequeathed us some of the best images of the city of London amidst the apocalypse of Martian tripods, Oesterheld left us an unforgettable panorama of a Buenos Aires conquered by alien forces.

DOI: 10.1057/9781137434371.0008

The first resistance group (Juan Salvo, his wife, his daughter and three friends, one of them a clever engineer called Favalli) insulate their home from the snow and with DIY (do-it-yourself) protective suits go out into the snow to look for food and weapons. According to Favalli, weapons were more important than food: 'The law of civilization was buried under the mortal snowfall'. While Elena and the little Martita remain at home, Salvo and his friends join a group of civilians and military men to take up arms against a powerful and unknown enemy.

Sasturain (1982, 1995), an Argentine author and literary critic who contributed to positioning *El Eternauta* in the broader context of the national popular narrative, wrote about the conception of the adventure and the everyday life in Oesterheld's *capolavoro*:

> Comparing everyday life to the openness of the new, the strange and surprising, Adventure becomes a privilege, a desirable and life-changing experience. But not the life of the conventional hero of classic adventure, of course, this character lives in the adventure, it is the air that he breathes, the landscape that surrounds him. Adventure changes life, it is a limit experience for those coming from 'normality', for the usual viewers of the exploits of others, transforming, by circumstances or chance, the subject of action [...] All the characters are revealed in the action and become heroes in the changing circumstances. (Sasturain, 1995, 111–119)

According to Juan Sasturain in Oesterheld's work the catalyst

> [...] is an extreme situation in which one can decide to choose or may choose between truth, meaning, or the bureaucratic alternative of doing nothing. And that is Oesterheld's hero. The hero does not exist before things happen, he doesn't have a particular physical skill or quality: he is a common man that the circumstances have tested and, in his reaction, he reveals to others and especially to himself that he is a hero [...] In Oesterheld the starting point is always everyday life: common life, the common man or boy, the emotions, his home, work, job, neighborhood, family, friends, free-time, and also his everyday routine. And then something happens to him, or he meets someone or something and there is a revelation that turns his life around, and it becomes something else. (Sasturain, 2012)

Oesterheld introduced a new figure into the narrative: the 'collective hero', a group of normal people fighting for survival and embodying strong values, from solidarity to loyalty.

Many researchers have found *El Eternauta* to be a source of reflection on storytelling in popular culture and media. Haywood Ferreira wrote

DOI: 10.1057/9781137434371.0008

that the first version of *El Eternauta* had 'universal as well as local appeal with its battle of good versus evil, the memorable resourcefulness of its characters, the multifaceted horrors of its alien creatures, and, most particularly, for its debunking of stereotypes' (2012, 156). Oesterheld played with the reader's assumptions about the hero and the alien. If traditional comics were (super)hero-centred, such as Superman, in *El Eternauta* Oesterheld proposed a collective hero made up of an organised group of normal citizens resisting the invasion. Moreover, if in traditional science fiction the technology is generally blamed for converting the city into a wasteland, *El Eternauta* described how 'Argentines use[d] technology in order to try to save their own city' (2012, 167). However, at the end of the comic an atomic attack from the northern superpowers destroy Buenos Aires. Juan Salvo, his family and a little group of survivors witness the annihilation of their city from a safe distance.

Another important component of *El Eternauta* is the invaders. After various different species of aliens (*cascarudos, gurbos, manos,* etc.) are described, the reader discovers that they are 'fellow victims forced to fight for a never seen race called *Los Ellos (The Them)*' (Ferreira, 2012, 157). Oesterheld recovered one of the basic principles of horror stories: the scariest monster is the one we never see.

El Eternauta is a sad story. Many survivors die during the resistance. Favalli ends up being transformed into a human-robot and reduced, like many others, to slavery. After the invaders destroy the city of Buenos Aires, Juan Salvo and his family try to escape in an alien vehicle. The alien technology is so impossible to decipher for a human mind that when Salvo pushes the button to turn the machine on, he finds himself alone in a space-time continuum. Salvo is now *El Eternauta,* a multidimensional traveller looking for his wife and daughter throughout time and space.

According to Ferreira,

> Latin Americanists and others who work with science fiction written in the periphery have since demonstrated that when science fiction icons are deployed away from their northern center of origin, they have a tendency to change or mutate as they are adapted to their environment. (2012, 156)

In this context Oesterheld made 'original use of classic science fiction icons, particularly those of the wasteland and the alien, with nods to the city and the robots' (155). To conclude we can say that in *El Eternauta* 'it is not physical power, superior weaponry, or even victory that

DOI: 10.1057/9781137434371.0008

determines human worthiness, but rather the will to resist and to fight for our beliefs' (171).

3.1.2   *El Eternauta* (1969)

The optimism about economic development and society's trust in the industrialisation strategies of the 1950s are evident in the first version of *El Eternauta*. Even the Argentine armed forces were part of the resistance movement: a group of military officers and soldiers organised the survivors and coordinated the first actions against the aliens. However, the Argentina of the late 1960s was a completely different country: the masses – not only in Argentina – were calling for a revolution. Che Guevara was already a combat flag and guerrillas were emerging all over the continent. Civil uprisings such as the *Cordobazo* and the *Rosariazo* (both in May 1969), general strikes and student and worker protests against the military government of General Onganía were part of everyday life. This is the context of the new version of *El Eternauta* written by Héctor Germán Oesterheld and illustrated by Alberto Breccia.

The new version published by the popular magazine *Gente* was darker – Breccia's experimental style was getting closer to Francisco Goya's *Black Paintings* (1819–1823) – and expressed a radical view of the political field. In this comic, Oesterheld made basic changes in the narrative: for example, the northern superpowers were allies with the aliens in the invasion of South America. Argentina had changed, Latin America had changed and Oesterheld had also changed: it would have been impossible to show military forces resisting the alien invasion in the late 1960s after the death of Guevara and the uprising of insurgent movements inspired by the Cuban revolution. The new *El Eternauta*, finally, was autobiographical: Germán (i.e. Oesterheld) is one of the main characters together with Juan Salvo.

This new version was too much for *Gente* magazine, a sunny publication with beautiful girls on the cover. The editor compelled Oesterheld and Breccia to abbreviate and finish the story in three weeks. The regularity of the narrative was definitively broken; it was almost impossible for Oesterheld to keep the rhythm of the original version: he just concluded the story following the path of the first edition.

Although this new version of *El Eternauta* was not as complete and regular as the first one, in the following years this comic was published in several European magazines such as *Linus, El Globo, Alter Alter, Il Mago,*

DOI: 10.1057/9781137434371.0008

Charlie Mensuel and *Metal Hurlant*. What Oesterheld could not tell at that time was filled in with Breccia's extended palette of blacks and greys.

3.1.3 *El Eternauta II* (1976) and beyond

After publishing a successful reissue of the 1957 version of *El Eternauta,* Ediciones Record asked Oesterheld for a second part of his *capolavoro.* In December 1975, Record started publishing *El Eternauta II* in *Skorpio* magazine, a sequel of the original story with artwork by Solano López. Once again Argentine history entered the story. In March 1976, military forces took over the government, arrested the President, Isabel Martínez de Perón, closed the Parliament and consolidated the political repression that had begun one year previously. The dictators responsible for the 30,000 *desaparecidos* and the future Falkland War (1982) had arrived to the command room.

Profoundly disturbed by the Dirty War and the political repression Oesterheld criticised the dictatorship in *El Eternauta II.* He introduced himself as a narrating character ('Germán') within the story and reflected deeply on survival in extreme conditions in a future inhospitable Argentina destroyed by invaders. At the same time Juan Salvo/ El Eternauta acquired supernatural powers and so became more like a typical North American comic-book superhero. According to Ferreira,

> [...] no longer content with the passive role of narrator in the outer frame of the story, Oesterheld/Germán becomes a main character in the central narrative itself, fighting alongside Juan Salvo as his right-hand man [...] There is a high price to pay for pressing *El Eternauta* into the service of a political cause. In addition to a widely acknowledged decline in the quality of the writing itself, this price can be seen most in the changes in the characterization of heroes and villains, good and evil, and in the more obvious delineation between them. (2012, 176)

Oesterheld and his daughters were already members of the revolutionary organisation Montoneros, and he wrote the new episodes of *El Eternauta II* from hidden locations in Buenos Aires. *El Eternauta II* was written and published under one of the bloodiest dictatorships in history. In 1977, a military task force kidnapped Oesterheld and he joined the list of *desaparecidos.* He is believed to have died some time after 1979, when he was last reported alive. His four daughters and two of their husbands also disappeared. Only his widow and two grandsons survived; the youngest boy was recovered from government custody after being born while his mother was in prison.

DOI: 10.1057/9781137434371.0008

Since 1983, with the return of democracy to Argentina, a series of sequels have been published together with different reprints of the older versions. With more or less success, the new comics expand the narrative world created by Oesterheld and López in the late 1950s. However, the original comic is unanimously considered a great science fiction story with an excellent balance between adventure, existential questions and human values mixed together in a solid popular media container.

The following table shows the entire comic narrative universe of *El Eternauta* produced by different artists over half a century:

TABLE 3.1   *Comic narrative universe of* El Eternauta

Year	Title	Writer	Illustrator
1957	*El Eternauta*	H.G.Oesterheld	Francisco Solano López
1969	*El Eternauta*	H.G.Oesterheld	Alberto Breccia
1976	*El Eternauta II*	H.G.Oesterheld	Francisco Solano López
1983	*El Eternauta: tercera parte*	Alberto Ongaro	Oswal and Mario Morhain
1997	*El Eternauta. El mundoarrepentido*	Pablo Maiztegui	Francisco Solano López
1999	*El Eternauta. Odiocósmico*	Pablo Muñoz and Ricardo Barreiro	Walther Taborda and Gabriel Rearte
2003	*El Eternauta. El regreso*	Pablo Maiztegui	Francisco Solano López
2006	*El Eternauta, el regreso. La búsqueda de Elena*	Pablo Maiztegui	Francisco Solano López
2007	*El Eternauta: El atajo. La batalla de la BibliotecaNacional*	Juan Sasturain	Francisco Solano López
2010	*El Eternauta: El perrollamador y otrashistorias*	Sergio Kern	Francisco Solano López, Salvador Sanz, Cristian Mallea and Enrique Santana
2010	*El Eternauta, el regreso: El fin del mundo*	Pablo Maiztegui	Francisco Solano López

3.2   *El Eternauta* and the transmedia promise

The image of *El Eternauta* has been an icon of popular resistance against dictatorships and military power for 30 years now. Many artists and producers have tried to adapt or expand the story to different media. Let us look at these productions, remembering that transmedia storytelling includes two characteristics: (1) the narrative expands across multiple media and platforms; and (2) users participate in the expansion by

DOI: 10.1057/9781137434371.0008

adding new texts (fan-fiction, parodies, recaps, alternate endings, etc.) to the narrative universe (Jenkins, 2003, 2006a, 2006b, 2009; Scolari, 2009a, 2012, 2013a, 2013b; Ibrus and Scolari, 2012; Jenkins, Ford and Green, 2013). In 1961, after closing Frontera, Oesterheld created a science-fiction magazine for Editorial Ramírez called *El Eternauta*. The following year Oesterheld published a novelised continuation of the comic; young artists like José Muñoz and Leopoldo Durañona illustrated each chapter (Oesterheld, 1995). The novel was based on episodes – like Ernie Pike´s *Unforgettable Battles* (Oesterheld-Pratt) or *Mort Cinder* (Oesterheld-Breccia) – that introduced historical events from the personal perspective of Juan Salvo/El Eternauta. Like Mort Cinder, the Eternauta witnesses many crucial moments of human history (i.e. the destruction of Pompeii, the nuclear attack on Hiroshima, etc.). After these historical explorations in issue 6, Oesterheld resumed *El Eternauta*. The continuation started in Tigre (Buenos Aires), continued in New York City and finished in an open conclusion in outer space (Oesterheld, 1995). According to Sasturain this sequel

> [...] jumps without transition from one climate to another, from one circumstance to another. It burns stages, modifies the rhythms on the way, passing from the details to the ellipses and often creates situations without developing all their possibilities. Like a draft hastily released where the lines of a story are embryonically developed, the story is thought of as it grows. There are at least four sequences. The first covers the adventures in El Tigre to meet Favalli; the second, the contact with the troops of Captain Timer and brief encounters with the enemy until heading north; the third is the experience of arrival and attack on New York City and ends with the fall of Salvo and Favalli, once again prisoners of the enemy; the fourth and inconclusive sequence (describes) the jump into outer space and the knowledge of a new perspective, a new galactic framework for the horrifying war [...] For the first time (Juan Salvo) lives the harsh law of the jungle – predicted by Favalli in the original story – as a single framework and pattern of relationship among the survivors. (Sasturain, 1995, 5–6)

Unfortunately only 15 issues (chapters) of this novel were published, and so the sequel of *El Eternauta* was left unfinished in February 1963.

As early as the late 1960s, a couple of spot producers tried to create a short animation movie with the support of Oesterheld but the project failed. Prestigious Argentine movie directors like Adolfo Aristarain, Fernando Solanas, Gustavo Mosquera and Lucrecia Martel have also considered the

DOI: 10.1057/9781137434371.0008

possibility of adapting *El Eternauta* to the big screen. Technical, financial and legal problems have stopped the project every time.

But the adaptations of *El Eternauta* have also explored other media beyond the screens and the books. In 1989 a group of radio professionals coordinated by Gustavo Arias and Patricio Apóstolo transformed *El Eternauta* into a radio play of 15 episodes each 12 minutes long, but it was never aired due to copyright issues (Apóstolo, s/d). In 1997 Jorge Morhain wrote a first adaptation for the theatre – El viajero de la eternidad – but it did not make it to the stage (Morhain, s/d). In 2003 the theatre company MorenaCanteroJrs. presented a new adaptation of Oesterheld's comic and in 2007 another group, Carne de Cañón, presented their work *Zona Liberada* inspired by *El Eternauta*. Three years later Radio Provincia de La Plata aired *El Eternauta: Vestigios del futuro*, a 22 episode adaptation directed by Martín Martinic Magan. Former versions had changed the name of the invader species to the name of the military men who had kidnapped Oesterheld. Finally, in 2011 there was a musical tribute to *El Eternauta* and H.G. Oesterheld entitled *Los Ellos* (*The Them*) with the participation of 17 music groups (all with different styles, from post-punk to psychedelic rock) and ten graphic artists. A documentary was also produced.

Although it has not been possible to produce a feature movie, considered from the perspective of contemporary transmedia storytelling research we can see how the official canon of *El Eternauta* has expanded from the original comic to different media (book, theatre and music). However, many of the most important transmedia extensions of *El Eternauta* can be found as user-generated contents.

3.3   From the Eternauta to the Nestornauta

On 27 October 2010, the former President of Argentina Néstor Kirchner (2003–2009) unexpectedly died from a heart attack. His death shocked Argentine society. Before the 2003 presidential election Kirchner was not a very well-known politician in Argentina – he was the governor of a remote province in Patagonia. Soon after arriving to government, Kirchner surprised the Argentines by standing down powerful military officials. Stressing the need to increase justice and democracy, Kirchner overturned amnesty laws for military officers accused of torture and assassinations during the 1976–1983 Dirty War. Kirchner showed himself to be concerned with the defence of human rights and in prosecuting

DOI: 10.1057/9781137434371.0008

those who had committed human rights violations during the Dirty War (later made immune from prosecution by the government of Carlos Menem between 1989 and 1999). Human rights organisations created during the dictatorship such as the Madres de Plaza de Mayo (*Mothers of the Plaza de Mayo*) and Abuelas de Plaza de Mayo (*Grandmothers of the Plaza de Mayo*) actively supported President Kirchner's policies.

3.3.1   Political appropriations

The death of President Kirchner in 2010 motivated the new generations into political participation after years of demobilisation. Thousands of young people joined political and social organisations after the crash of 2001 but they only emerged as relevant public actors after Kirchner's death.

FIGURE 3.1   *Graffiti of th-*
Source: ©Leonar.

In August 2010, a few months before Kirchner's death, a Peronist group organised a political meeting for the new generations and proposed that they use a new image: a remix of the traditional image of Juan Salvo/El Eternauta and Néstor Kirchner. It is in this context that the *Nestornauta* was born. The Nestornauta was officially presented in the political meeting held at Luna Park (14 September 2010) under the slogan 'Néstor le habla a la juventud, la juventud le habla a Néstor' ('Néstor talks to young people, young people talk to Néstor'). The organisation produced three posters: the first one was inspired by the traditional aesthetics of the Peronist movement, the second one adopted Andy Warhol's pop art style (!) and the third one was the *Nestornauta* (Fernández and Gago, 2012, 122).

The *Nestornauta* has the body of Juan Salvo with his biohazard suit as shown in the original comic but with the face of Néstor Kirchner. One important detail: the *Nestornauta* is not carrying a rifle on his back. New political groups like La Cámpora – one of the most active organisations of the new generation – distributed stencils so the image could be spray-painted onto Argentine walls. But that's not all. Following a long-standing tradition a dummy of the Nestornauta was burned on 31 December 2011 in La Plata by the Megafón Commando, a group of young followers of the Peronist movement (ComandoMegafón, 2012). The artist Ignacio Brizzio has also produced a series of small sculptures representing Perón, Evita and the *Nestornauta* (Di Nucci, 2013).

An intertextual note before continuing. In 2001, during one of the worst crises in Argentine history, an image of Juan Salvo/Eternauta with Héctor G. Oesterheld's face appeared on many walls and banners. A single word accompanied these images: *Resist*. As we can see it is possible to identify a intertextual network or semiological chain that starts with the original Eternauta character in the 1950s and 1960s, follows with the face of Oesterheld in 2001 (*Oesternauta*) and expands with new versions now involving Néstor Kirchner (*Nestornauta*).

3.3.2   Academic interpretations

This mu~~...~~tion of a fictional character into a political icon in the context of the political ~~...~~ of the Kirchnerist movement has generated many analyses, debate~~...~~ of the controversies (Aguirre, 2012, Fernández and Gago, 2012; Larrondo, 2013; ~~...~~012; Montero and Vincent, 2013; Reggiani, 2011). Some researchers ~~...~~ed out the contradictions

In August 2010, a few months before Kirchner's death, a Peronist group organised a political meeting for the new generations and proposed that they use a new image: a remix of the traditional image of Juan Salvo/El Eternauta and Néstor Kirchner. It is in this context that the *Nestornauta* was born. The Nestornauta was officially presented in the political meeting held at Luna Park (14 September 2010) under the slogan 'Néstor le habla a la juventud, la juventud le habla a Néstor' ('Néstor talks to young people, young people talk to Néstor'). The organisation produced three posters: the first one was inspired by the traditional aesthetics of the Peronist movement, the second one adopted Andy Warhol's pop art style (!) and the third one was the *Nestornauta* (Fernández and Gago, 2012, 122).

The *Nestornauta* has the body of Juan Salvo with his biohazard suit as shown in the original comic but with the face of Néstor Kirchner. One important detail: the *Nestornauta* is not carrying a rifle on his back. New political groups like La Cámpora – one of the most active organisations of the new generation – distributed stencils so the image could be spray-painted onto Argentine walls. But that's not all. Following a long-standing tradition a dummy of the Nestornauta was burned on 31 December 2011 in La Plata by the Megafón Commando, a group of young followers of the Peronist movement (ComandoMegafón, 2012). The artist Ignacio Brizzio has also produced a series of small sculptures representing Perón, Evita and the *Nestornauta* (Di Nucci, 2013).

An intertextual note before continuing. In 2001, during one of the worst crises in Argentine history, an image of Juan Salvo/Eternauta with Héctor G. Oesterheld's face appeared on many walls and banners. A single word accompanied these images: *Resist*. As we can see it is possible to identify a intertextual network or semiological chain that starts with the original Eternauta character in the 1950s and 1960s, follows with the face of Oesterheld in 2001 (*Oesternauta*) and expands with new versions now involving Néstor Kirchner (*Nestornauta*).

3.3.2   Academic interpretations

This mutation of a fictional character into a political icon in the context of the political discourse of the Kirchnerist movement has generated many analyses, debates and controversies (Aguirre, 2012, Fernández and Gago, 2012; Larrondo, 2013; Montero, 2012; Montero and Vincent, 2013; Reggiani, 2011). Some researchers have pointed out the contradictions

DOI: 10.1057/9781137434371.0008

those who had committed human rights violations during the Dirty War (later made immune from prosecution by the government of Carlos Menem between 1989 and 1999). Human rights organisations created during the dictatorship such as the Madres de Plaza de Mayo (*Mothers of the Plaza de Mayo*) and Abuelas de Plaza de Mayo (*Grandmothers of the Plaza de Mayo*) actively supported President Kirchner's policies.

3.3.1   Political appropriations

The death of President Kirchner in 2010 motivated the new generations into political participation after years of demobilisation. Thousands of young people joined political and social organisations after the crash of 2001 but they only emerged as relevant public actors after Kirchner's death.

FIGURE 3.1   *Graffiti of the Nestornauta*
Source: ©Leonardo Samrani

DOI: 10.1057/9781137434371.0008

between the original character and the new version; others have focused on the different appropriation of *El Eternauta* before and after the death of Néstor Kirchner. According to Reggiani, there is a mismatch between the figure of *El Eternauta* and Néstor Kirchner.

> [...] *El Eternauta* is the story of a struggle of resistance against the State. It is, in a consistent way, an anti-State fiction. The invasion ends with the destruction of the Argentine National Government, and their remains (the army) only survive to demonstrate their failure. Foreign states also fail – they atomized Buenos Aires only after the partisans Juan, Franco and Favalli destroyed the core of the invasion – or, in Breccia's 1969 version, after they betray the Third World. And The Them are, even in their invisible presence, a State. A state that rules by coercion and terror [...] Salvo and his friends face the most absolute version of a State. (Reggiani, 2011)

Fernández and Gago (2012) analyzed the double appropriation of *El Eternauta*. Before Kirchner's death, the character was considered a cultural and political icon of the popular 'resistance' and 'sacrifice'. After October 2010, the myth was re-signified transforming Néstor Kirchner into a hero who gave his life for a political project. The *Nestornauta* is one of strongest symbolic connections between the new generation and the political movements of the early 1970s. In this context the *Nestornauta* works as a bridge between two political times (and societies): the Argentina of the 1970s and the Argentina of the 2010s. According to Fernández and Gago,

> There is a different intention in the use of the Eternauta image before and after the death of Néstor Kirchner; the latter case explicitly searches for parallels in the idea of the heroic sacrifice between the character, the writer and politician, in an empathetic operation oriented towards the young militants. In this operation the hybridization of languages and aesthetics was key, as well as mediation of new technologies and media for the creation, circulation and reception of political messages. (2012, 126)

The debate around the *Nestornauta* was not only limited to social science journals and books: the pages of the press also joined in. An article published by Osvaldo Aguirre in *La Capital* (2012) is a good example of these exchanges:

> Lautaro Ortiz (comic editor): The interpretation proposed by the followers of Kirchner 'is not different from Oesterheld's own interpretation [...] For the first time a political group proposes and activates an interpretation of history from a popular art like the comic [...] The Kirchnerist movement did not

DOI: 10.1057/9781137434371.0008

invent anything. They did not alter or deform the work. They just massified an interpretation and disseminated it at a critical time like this one. In any case, they set it up as an example of how a man must live in community life. Always as a whole'. (in Aguirre, 2012).

Lautaro Cossia (researcher): 'Every consolidated or emergent political construction feeds on symbols that work as a brand identity that connects them with a tradition of fights, schools of thought and social values'. (in Aguirre, 2012)

Marcos Novaro (sociologist): The *Nestornauta* 'is a mythical construction for domestic consumption of the ruling party. The Nestornauta has the potential to mobilize within their own people, it is a device, a partisan political resource that aligns the ranks, but does not recruit, it does not add new ones [...] The myth is feeble because Néstor (Kirchner) was a guy who never took risks, [...] he always remained on the midline. He was the prototype of the politician who takes no risks, the Eternauta has nothing to do with that'. (in Aguirre, 2012)

Judith Gociol (co-author of *La Historieta Argentina. Una historia*): 'What is happening today is an addition of contemporary political overtones to a school of thought that since the 70s has placed *El Eternauta* and Oesterheld's intellectual trajectory within the national and popular tradition, particularly his approach to the Peronist left and the conversion of his works into a militant gesture'. (in Aguirre, 2012)

According to Laura Fernández, a young researcher and artist, the appropriation of *El Eternauta* is consistent with the general discourse of Kirchnerism

In the last phase of his life Oesterheld sympathized with the left wing of Peronism. We must recognize that Kichnerism is the closest thing to that Peronism, at least since the beginning of democracy (1983), with all the possible criticisms. Additionally, *El Eternauta II* is clearly linked to Montonero's discourse, therefore the *Eternéstor* or *Nestornauta* is no aberration, besides being an appropriation it refers to a link, and not at all a distant link, since rescuing that period is what they are trying to do today. And Néstor Kirchner was a president who clearly decided to create a bridge with that experience. (Fernández, 2012)

In 2012 a group of young members of the Kirchnerist movement, with the support of the Ministry of Education, introduced a game based on *El Eternauta* into schools. Although many people welcomed the initiative – the universal social and moral values of *El Eternauta* are beyond debate – others considered that political activity was invading the classrooms. According to Novaro,

DOI: 10.1057/9781137434371.0008

The problem is not the political activity into the schools, but the political activity of the State entering schools. One thing is that students are mobilized and another one that a guy from the Cabinet campaigns with a game of a collective hero [...] Supposedly the game has a civic purpose but it is used as a cover for a political campaign to promote the official creeds and insult the opponents. It is a partisan activity driven from the State into the schools, something very different from a youth activity. (in Aguirre, 2012)

As it can be seen, in Argentina *El Eternauta* and his political offspring – el *Nestornauta* – are at the centre of contemporary political debates and conflicts. If some intellectuals consider it a clumsy political move, for many others the different embodiments of *El Eternauta* represent the continuity of a political tradition. An online publication by young militants summarised this former interpretation:

Oesterheld and his creation are symbols of the noblest hopes of our history, but also of its most nefarious and bloodthirsty side. His figure, painted on the walls, represents this double dimension where the dreams of a better world converge with the worst horrors that those who dare to fight for their dreams can receive. It is known that people express their stories in symbols. (Juan) Salvo in his wetsuit marching through the snow, facing the horror, staring forward, ready to continue the struggle, is just a good example of that. (Cladakis and Bergna, 2010)

3.4   Transmedia storytelling and political movements

According to political discourse analysts Verón and Sigal,

Any political discourse [...] contains the recovery of history as one of its fundamental dimensions. Every political position reconstructs the story in its own way, in order to root the social movement or party into the logic of a development and demonstrate that they are 'necessary'. The story appears, then, as a metaphor of the present. (1986, 182)

Political discourses do not only recover history: they also re-appropriate narrative fictional worlds. Fictions offer a set of environments, characters and stories that are very useful for developing political discourses. In 2010 a group of Palestinian, Israeli and international activists painted themselves blue to resemble the Na'vi characters from James Cameron's *Avatar*. The activists marched along the Israeli West Bank barrier until they were intercepted by the Israeli military. The parallelism with the Na'vi struggles to defend their green planet against the military-industrial

DOI: 10.1057/9781137434371.0008

complex were evident. The video of the repression ended up on YouTube,[2] where more than 250,000 users have watched it.

> As the image of the Na'vi has been taken up by protest groups in various parts of the world, the myth has instead been rewritten to focus on local embodiments of the military-industrial complex. In Bil'in, the focus was on the Israeli army; in China, it was on the struggles of homeowners against land seizures by developers working with the Chinese government; in Brazil, it was the Amazon Indians against dam construction threatening the rain forest; and, in London, it was activists protesting British mining interests on behalf of a tribe in India. (Jenkins, Ford and Green, 2013, parag. 601)

Transmedia storytelling and user-generated contents propose a new model for activism, one that is 'both spectacular and participatory, drawing emotional power from stories that already matter to a mass public' (Jenkins, Ford and Green, 2013, parag. 603). The '*Avatar* operation' simplified the identification of the Other-Invader and the viral diffusion of the video at a global scale, going beyond the core audience already invested in this conflict. Everybody knows who the bad guys are in *Avatar*.

In the specific case of the Peronist movement, throughout its history this movement, created by Juan Domingo Perón in the 1940s, identified many enemies, from US Imperialism to Communism. Similar to any other political movement the construction of the Other has been a permanent sense production device in its discourse. The identification of an enemy has a double function: to bring together the movement's own forces and, at the same time, draw a borderline that identifies the presence of hostile forces beyond it. It could be said that any political or social actor produces a narrative that recognises 'friends' and 'enemies'.

The arrival of Néstor Kirchner to the presidency of Argentina in 2003 opened a new discursive phase characterised by the recovery of the memory of the 1970s revolutionary movements. This appropriation of the past re-signified a series of narratives, topics and values from the 1970s (*sacrifice, resistance, anti-imperialism, popular unity, revolution*, etc.). Fictions like *El Eternauta* embody these values. At the same time, this discursive movement recovered and upgraded the figure of the Other, now an enemy represented by a block that combines neoliberalism and authoritarianism. But as many discourse analysts have demonstrated, the discourse of Kirchnerism also includes elements that originate in other political traditions, from republicanism to liberalism (Montero, 2012, 259–282).

DOI: 10.1057/9781137434371.0008

The sequence *Eternauta-Oesternauta-Nestornauta* should be understood as a continuity of a (voluntary or not) *sacrifice*. After Kirchner's death many political and social leaders stated that 'Néstor Kirchner gave his life for his country' (Hebe de Bonafini – Mothers of Plaza de Mayo, 23 March 2011) or 'Kirchner gave his life for his country [...] he was indispensable' (Estela de Carlotto – Grandmothers of Plaza de Mayo, 27 October 2010) (in Fernández and Gago, 2012, 123). One of the most interesting things about *El Eternauta* is that the appropriation of this character started at the periphery of the political system but it was eventually used by its most important enunciator: the State. The different appropriations of the character (from the *Eternauta* to the *Nestornauta*, going through the *Oesternauta*) and the tensions between peripheral and central political enunciators are representative of the complexity of textual sense production and interpretation processes.

Finally, it must be said that transmedia storytelling goes beyond the interests and intentions of the media corporations. According to the Argentine writer Ricardo Piglia (2014), 'a story is not interpreted: it is retold. We can also understand the cultural tradition as a system of replicated, cancelled, criticized, and folded narratives. The stories do not close the meaning, they lead (people) to think'. In this context it is relatively easy to identify where a transmedia narrative world begins (a feature movie, a novel, a comic) but it is almost impossible to know where it ends.

Notes

1   Mort Cinder is an enigmatic man who comes back from the grave each time he dies. His partner is Winston, an antique dealer. Cinder has lived since ancient times and has taken part in many famous historical episodes, including the building of the tower of Babel, World War I and the battle of Thermopylae. This immortal character has many connections to Jack London's novel *The Star Rover* (1915) and Jorge Luis Borges short stories (i.e. *The Immortal*, 1949). However, the main traits of Cinder are human and not supernatural.

2   *BilinReenacts Avatar Film 12-02-2010* by Haitham Al Katib, https://www.youtube.com/watch?v=Chw32qG-M7E date accessed 20 April 2014.

DOI: 10.1057/9781137434371.0008

Conclusions: Transmedia Storytelling and Popular Cultures in the Twentieth Century

Carlos A. Scolari, Paolo Bertetti and Matthew Freeman

Abstract: *This chapter presents the main conclusions of the book and highlights the profound difficulty faced by researchers when attempting to map, define, trace and fully understand transmedia narrative experiences. The chapter aims to demonstrate how transmedia storytelling has been not only a narrative practice but also a social one across a range of historical moment, emerging as a basic component of popular culture in the twentieth century and even before.*

Keywords: narrative expansion; pulp fiction; seriality; Superman; transmedia storytelling; world-building

Scolari, Carlos A., Paolo Bertetti, and Matthew Freeman. *Transmedia Archaeology: Storytelling in the Borderlines of Science Fiction, Comics and Pulp Magazines.* Basingstoke: Palgrave Macmillan, 2014. DOI: 10.1057/9781137434371.0009.

DOI: 10.1057/9781137434371.0009

The permeation of transmedia storytelling through popular culture, its longevity, its complexity, and its flexibility amidst cultural influences, highlights the profound difficulty faced by researchers when attempting to map, define, trace and fully understand these narrative experiences. The three case studies explored in this book provide a useful starting point for illustrating the multiplication of transmedia storytelling as a practice in all its various forms and manifestations across different historical periods and geographical contexts. In so far as the tales of *Conan the Barbarian*, *Superman*, and *El Eternauta* all begin in one medium and expand across an array of surrounding media platforms, with their fans participating in the active creation of the fictional world, they are all, to some degree, typical of what we now understand as transmedia storytelling. Yet their creation as part of diverse historical settings – influenced not by a moment of convergence but rather by pulp formats and political crises of the past – means that these case studies are also atypical of our understanding of transmedia storytelling.

Despite his enduring popularity, the origins of *Conan the Barbarian*, for instance, are deeply rooted in the pulp formats and aesthetic. His creator, Robert Howard, was a prolific author who published his stories in many different kinds of pulp, and Conan was intentionally created as a series character to be inserted in to many different stories. All his original adventures appeared almost in continuity on the pages of the same magazine, *Weird Tales*, one of the most legendary of the pulp era.

Even so, Conan's transmedia expansion across media began relatively late, due to the lack of popular interest in fantasy and sword & sorcery genres during the 1950s and the first half of 1960s. The character's first appearance in comic books hails from the 1970s, and he was required to wait until the 1980s before debuting in film and the 1990s to arrive on television. Nevertheless, his development as a character shows that some dynamics, such as the centrality of world-building and the fans participative practices, each usually associated with modern transmedia storytelling, were already operating in the dynamics of narrative expansion of pulp literature of the 1930s. In particular, the creation of a fictional world was typical of fantasy and sword & sorcery, and generally a result of the aesthetics of the pulps. In Howard's Conan adventures, one shared fictional universe was common, albeit in different eras, with different characters and stories: Kull, Conan, Bran Mac Morn and other Howard's characters all refer to a single imaginary and mythical history of our world. On the other hand, as we have seen in chapter 1, Conan is one of

DOI: 10.1057/9781137434371.0009

the first examples where fans had a key role in the narrative development of the character, participating equally in the ways that formed the 'canon' of Conan, in turn promoting the first outlining of the life history of the Barbarian, only afterwards being corrected by Howard.

Superman, much like Conan the Barbarian before him, was a character born out of a particular pulp heritage. The fiction factories of the early twentieth century, spawning stories of adventure, mystery, science fiction and fantasy, had made a habit of narrating the adventures of their heroes across countless editions of magazines. The stories extended, the worlds expanded, and in time the practices of world-creation and world-expansion at the heart of pulp fiction materialised in surrounding media, bringing with them new avenues to extend and expand fiction across a whole host of available media. Built around strategies of seriality, narrative expansion and implication, and further properties of world-building, Superman's comic storyworld was built in the late 1930s and continued to expand throughout the 1940s via a careful use of such pulp-orientated arsenal. Fans had begun to collaborate with the Superman world, attending special events and fairs based around the character in ways that fortified further consumer-driven expansions. New features of the storyworld were added in newspaper strips, new characters added and narrated across multiple comic books, while the storyworld itself expanded to tie in related characters and storyworlds such as Batman and Wonder Woman.

Narrative arsenal such as this, once closely associated with the pulp productions of Conan, Tarzan, Zorro, and The Shadow, became effective tools for serialising narratives and expanding storyworlds in other media, too. Radio quickly adopted models of seriality and anthology formats; cinema began to experiment with the serial form and related strategies of integrating with surrounding media outlets. With media forms adopting and cross-pollinating many of the same storytelling models and practices, utilising pre-formed audiences more and more, adopting pre-sold genre types with more frequency, it is understandable as to why certain characters, stories and storyworlds themselves began to cross media with ease. Only by inheriting the narrative strategies of this historical period's oft-maligned and marginalised pulp fictions did transmedia storytelling therefore evolve into a cross-industrial practice of many of the adjacent media industries. As Roger T. Reed concludes of the pulps, 'precisely because these phenomena were fringe phenomena, at the edges of culture, they helped define its overall shape' (1997, 8).

DOI: 10.1057/9781137434371.0009

Pulp magazines, dwindling in the outer niche of popular culture in the twentieth century, served as something of a transitional stepping stone in the cultural history of entertainment production – the cultures, practices and usages of pulp fictions, as Edgar Rice Burroughs had once described, were indeed nothing if not stepping stones of entertainment, unravelling across multiple media forms.

El Eternauta, meanwhile, was also a comic character but one transformed into an icon of popular resistance against one of the bloodiest dictatorships of contemporary history. Even if the official expansions of the story have been limited and in many cases never went beyond the prototype – we have identified novels, animations, radio, theatre and music – the transition from the Eternauta to the Nestornauta confirms once more the unlimited capacity of users for resignifying, remixing and producing new creative contents. What the producer can't do, doesn't want to do or doesn't know how to do will be done by the prosumers.

The debates and conflicts generated by the political appropriation of *El Eternauta* are a good example of the cultural processes that transmedia storytelling may generate. If many scholars and professionals still think that 'transmedia storytelling' is a fashionable concept coming from Hollywood, the resignification of Oesterheld's character shows that transmedia practices go beyond the producer's commercial interests and strategies and involve many processes beyond their control.

In the specific case of *El Eternauta*, the new character conveys the same values (sacrifice, resistance, fight, loyalty, etc.) in a different context, creating a link with political processes developed in the 1960s and 1970s. The arrival of the Nestornauta triggered a series of discourses that support or go against a political strategy. If we compare the appropriation of El Eternauta with other experiences – such as the appropriation of *Avatar*'s characters in Palestine (Jenkins, Ford and Green, 2013) – there is a big difference: in the Argentine case, the reappropriation was born into a specific sector of a political party but was immediately adopted by the State. In both cases the recovering of fictional characters and narratives facilitated the identification of enemies/allies and ensured a viral circulation of the discourse.

Altogether it is therefore important to reiterate a clear but important point: transmedia storytelling is not new. We have seen throughout this book how transmedia storytelling has been not only a narrative practice but also a social one across a range of historical moments, emerging as a basic component of popular culture in the twentieth century and even

DOI: 10.1057/9781137434371.0009

before. Of course, as also acknowledged in the Introduction, protesting to unveil the full history of transmedia storytelling is far beyond the scope of our aims here. Further research should continue to be done to expand the reconstruction of the origins of transmedia narrative worlds (Freeman, 2014a; Freeman, 2014b; Scolari, 2014).

In beginning the discussion on the archaeology of transmedia, however, our work here has highlighted the importance of pulp fiction – pulp magazines and comics – on the evolution of transmedia storytelling. In the twentieth century pulp fiction such as that explored throughout this book was the prime example of seriality, preceding the arrival of television series. In particular, comics were the field of popular culture where a number of questions common to transmedia storytelling emerged with major evidence, such as those concerning the continuity of narratives across editions, or those concerning the consistency of the shared diegetic universe. Moreover, many theoretical models used to understand transmedia storytelling – be them ideas of interstitial microstories that fill the gaps in the macrostory (Scolari, 2009a), or less formal ideas such as the stepping stones of entertainment suggested in chapter 2 – are all applicable and suitable to the pulps and comics mode of storytelling.

Relatedly, the role of particular genre types on transmedia fictions emerges as another key underlying factor. Though *Conan the Barbarian*, *Superman* and *El Eternauta* each borrow from slightly different sub-genres – stretching from heroic fantasy to superhero to science fiction, each overlapping to varying degrees – the overall framework of fantasy/ science fiction is thus true for all three. Even today, these particular genres continue to remain key for transmedia storytelling – framing the worlds and narrative actions of *The Matrix*, *Star Wars*, *Doctor Who*, *Lost*, *Heroes*, *Harry Potter*, and so on. Structurally and thematically, fantasy and science fiction seem to afford ample world-creation possibilities. As we have seen, science fiction explores possible or parallel worlds; the outward-looking nature of these genres may often work as a structural necessity to create a detailed world for the inner (fictional) reference, continuing to expand across multiple texts across multiple media, as described in chapter 2.

In the age of the digital, we have come to expect fans not only to produce 'contents' but also to actively participate in the construction of the narrative canon. Even in the historical settings explored throughout this book, the same is true to some extent. Audiences participated in the

DOI: 10.1057/9781137434371.0009

worlds of *Conan the Barbarian, Superman* and *El Eternauta* in different ways, shaping narratives and prosuming texts. Fan cultures had been developing rapidly in the 1930s around science fiction conventions and memorabilia fairs, encouraging this sort of active, transmedial engagement between audiences and producers.

Transmedia storytelling hereby emerges as a useful testing bench for fields such as semiotics, fandom and narratology across a whole range of historical and geographic contexts. In so far as the research on transmedia narrative worlds promotes a generation of new analytical categories as well as a general improvement to academic theories about storytelling and (inter)textual networks, we hope that this book intersects across these networks, opening up new conceptual territory about such phenomena.

DOI: 10.1057/9781137434371.0009

References

O. Aguirre (2012) 'Los mitos de la historieta argentina', *La Capital,* 9 September, http://www.lacapital.com. ar/ed_senales/2012/9/edicion_190, date accessed 23 April 2014.

P. Apóstolo (s/d) El Eternauta: una visión radial sobre guiones de Héctor G. Oesterheld para la historieta del mismo nombre, http://www.portalcomic.com (home page), date accessed 23 April 2014.

T. Balio (1995) *Grand Design: Hollywood as a Modern Business Enterprise, 1930-1939* (Berkeley, CA: University of California Press).

R. Barthes (1968) 'L'effet du réel', *Communications,* 11, 84–89.

R. Barthes (1970) *S/Z* (Paris, France: Seuil).

P. Bertetti (2011) *Conan il mito* (Pisa, Italy: ETS).

P. Bertetti (2014) 'Toward a Typology of Transmedia Characters', *International Journal of Communication,* 8, 2344–2361. http://ijoc.org/index.php/ijoc/article/ view/2597, date accessed 15 September 2014, doi 1932–8036/20140005.

P. Booth (2010) *Digital Fandom: New Media Studies* (New York, NY: Peter Lang).

E. R. Burroughs (20 December 1912) [Letter courtesy of Edgar Rice Burroughs, Inc.].

F. Casetti (1984) 'Introduzione' in F. Casetti (eds.) L'immagine al plurale. Serialità e ripetizione nel cinema e nella televisione, pp. 7-18 (Venezia, Italy: Marsilio).

M. Cladakis and E. Bergna (2010) 'El Nestornauta, caminante de la eternidad', *Ágora. A diario la arena*

DOI: 10.1057/9781137434371.0010

política, http://agoraadiario.blogspot.com.es (home page), date accessed 23 April 2014.

M. J. Clarke (2009) 'Lost and Mastermind Narration', *Television and New Media*, 11(2), 123–142.

M. J. Clarke (2013) *Transmedia Television: New Trends in Network Serial Production* (New York, NY: Bloomsbury).

A. Clayton (2012) 'A. Evolution and Race on the Island of Caspak: How Tarzan and T-Rex Decode Manhood in the Comic that Time Forgot' in A. Wannamaker and M. A. Abate (eds) *Global Perspectives on Tarzan: From King of the Jungle to International Icon* (New York, Routledge), 180–197.

J. Coma (1984) *El ocaso del héroe en el comic de autor* (Barcelona, Spain: Península).

ComandoMegafón (2012) 'La quema de Nestornauta desde La Plata, Ciudad Evita', *ComandoMegafón* (blog), 5 January, http://comandomegafon.blogspot.com.es(home page), date accessed 23 April 2014.

N. Couldry (2011) 'More Sociology, More Culture, More Politics. Or, a Modest Proposal for 'Convergence' Studies', *Cultural Studies*, 25(4/5), 487–501. doi:10.1080/09502386.2011.600528

J. Courtés (1986) *Le conte populaire: poétique et mythologie* (Paris, France: PUF).

T. DeForest (2004) *Storytelling in the Pulps, Comics, and Radio: How Technology Changed Popular Fiction in America* (London, UK: McFarland & Company).

C. Dena (2009) *Transmedia practice: Theorising the practice of expressing a fictional world across distinct media and environments.* unpublished PhD thesis, University of Sydney, Australia, http://dl.dropbox.com/u/30158/DENA_TransmediaPractice.pdf, date accessed 4 August 2014.

S. Di Nucci (2013) 'Miniaturas Nac & Pop para coleccionar', *TiempoArgentino*, 12 December, http://tiempo.infonews.com(home page), date accessed 25 April 2014.

L. Dolezel (1998) *Heterocosmics: Fiction and Possible Words* (Baltimore, MD: John Hopkins University Press).

U. Eco (1979) *Lector in Fabula* (Milano, Italy: Bompiani).

U. Eco (1984) *Semiotica e filosofia del linguaggio* (Torino, Italy: Einaudi). English translation: *Semiotics and the Philosophy of Language*, Bloomington, IN: Indiana University Press, 1986.

DOI: 10.1057/9781137434371.0010

U. Eco (1985) 'Innovation and Repetition: Between Modern and Post-Modern Aesthetics', *Daedalus*, 114(4), 161–184.

U. Eco (1994) *Six Walks in the Fictional Woods* (Cambridge, MA: Harvard University Press).

L. Elleström (2010) *Media Borders, Multimodality and Intermediality* (Houndmills, UK: Palgrave Macmillan).

E. Evans (2011) *Transmedia Television. Audiences, New Media and Daily Life* (New York, NY: Routledge).

(9 February 1914) *Moving Picture World*.

L. Fernández (2012) 'El Nestornauta no es una aberración. Interview by Maria Eva Guevara', *Veintitrés*, 12 December, http://veintitres.infonews.com(home page), date accessed 25 April 2014.

L. Fernández and S. Gago (2012) 'Historieta y mitos políticos: la relectura oficial de El Eternauta en la Argentina democrática', *Anagramas*, 10(20), 117–128.

M. Finn (2006) *Blood and Thunder: The Life and Art of Robert E. Howard* (Austin, TX: Monkeybrain Books).

M. Freeman (2014a) 'Branding Consumerism: Cross-media Characters and Story-worlds at the Turn of the 20th Century', *The International Journal of Cultural Studies*, January 2014, http://ics.sagepub.com (home page), date accessed 6 April 2014. doi: 10.1177/1367877913515868

M. Freeman (2014b) 'Advertising the Yellow Brick Road: Historicizing the Industrial Emergence of Transmedia Storytelling', *International Journal of Communication*, 8, 2362–2381, http://ijoc.org/index.php/ijoc/article/view/2486, date accessed 15 September 2014, doi 1932 -8036/20140005.

S. Ford (2006a) *As the world turns in a convergence culture*. Master's dissertation, Comparative Media Studies, MIT, http://cms.mit.edu/research/theses/SamFord2007.pdf, date accessed 22 May 2013.

S. Ford (2007b) 'Immersive Story-Worlds Part One', *Confessions of an Aca-Fan: The Official Weblog of Henry Jenkins*, http://henryjenkins.org (home page), date accessed 22 May 2013.

D. Geeraerts, Dirk (1989) 'Prospects and problems of prototype theory', *Linguistics*, 27(4), 587–612.

B. K. Grant (2004) 'Sensuous Elaboration: Reason and the Visible in the Science Fiction Film', Redmond, S. *Liquid Metal: The Science Fiction Film Reader* (London, UK: Wallflower Press).

W. G. Gray (2000) *The Conan Timeline*, http://www.barbariankeep.com/galen.html, date accessed 22 March 2014.

DOI: 10.1057/9781137434371.0010

W. G. Gray and B. Precourt (2005) *The Complete Conan Bibliography*, http://conan.com/bibliography.shtml, date accessed 22 March 2014.

A. J. Greimas and J. Courtés (1979) *Sémiotique. Dictionnaire raisonné de la théorie du langage* (Paris, France: Hachette).

A. J. Greimas (1983). *Du sens II* (Paris, France: Seuil).

M. Grishanova and M.-L. Ryan (2010) *Intermediality and Storytelling* (Berlin, Germany: De Gruyter).

G. Grossman (1977) *Superman: Serial to Cereal* (New York, NY: The Popular Library Film Series).

R. Hagedorn (1988) 'Technology and Economic Exploitation: The Serial as a Form of Narrative Presentation', *Wide Angle*, 10.

Ph. Hamon (1977) 'Pour un statut sémiologique du personnage' in VV. AA., *Poétique du récit* (Paris, France: Seuil).

J. Hay and N. Couldry (2011) 'Rethinking Convergence/Culture', *Cultural Studies*, 25(4–5), 473–486. doi:10.1080/09502386.2011.600527

R. Haywood Ferreira (2010) 'MásAllá, El Eternauta, and the Dawn of the Golden Age of Latin American Science Fiction (1953–59)', *Extrapolation*, 51(2), 281–303.

R. Haywood Ferreira (2012) 'Oesterhelds's Iconic and Ironic Eternautas', in M. E. Ginway and J. A. Brown (eds) *Latin American Science Fiction: Theory and Practice*, 155–184 (New York, NY: Palgrave MacMillan).

M. Hills (2002) *Fan Cultures* (New York, NY: Routledge).

I. Ibrus, and C. A. Scolari (eds) (2012) *Crossmedia Innovations: Texts, Markets, Institutions* (Frankfurt, Germany: Peter Lang).

(19 January 1920) *The Film Daily*.

(3 July 1940) *The Film Daily*, 180.

(7 January 1923) Creator of Tarzan Speaks. *Los Angeles Times*.

(9 January 1948) Col Shapes 'Superman' Into Cliffhanger. *Variety*.

H. Jenkins (2003) 'Transmedia Storytelling: Moving Characters from Books to Films to Video Games Can Make Them Stronger and More Compelling', *Technology Review*, 15 January, http://www.technologyreview.com (home page), date accessed 15 January 2014.

H. Jenkins (2006a) *Convergence Culture: Where Old and New Media Collide* (New York, NY: New York University Press).

H. Jenkins (2006b) *Fans, Bloggers, and Gamers: Exploring Participatory Culture* (New York, NY: New York University Press).

H. Jenkins (2008) 'I Have Seen the Future of Entertainment ... And It Works', *Confessions of an Aca-Fan: The Official Weblog of Henry Jenkins*, http://henryjenkins.org (home page), date accessed 30 November 2013.

DOI: 10.1057/9781137434371.0010

H. Jenkins (2009) 'The Revenge of the Origami Unicorn: Seven Principles of Transmedia Storytelling', *Confessions of an Aca-Fan: The Official Weblog of Henry Jenkins*, http://henryjenkins.org (home page), date accessed 15 January 2014.

H. Jenkins (2011) 'Transmedia 202: Further Reflections', *Confessions of an Aca-Fan: The Official Weblog of Henry Jenkins*, http://henryjenkins.org (home page), date accessed 21 May 2013.

H. Jenkins (2014) 'Transmedia: A Prehistory' in D. Mann (ed.) *Wire TV: Laboring over an Interactive Future* (New York, NY: Rutgers University Press).

H. Jenkins, and M. Deuze, (2008) 'Editorial. Convergence culture', *Convergence: The International Journal of Research into New Media Technologies*, 14(1), 5–12.

H. Jenkins, S. Ford and J. Green (2013) *Spreadable Media: Creating Value and Meaning in a Networked Culture* (New York, NY: New York University Press).

D. Johnson (2013) *Media Franchising: Creative License and Collaboration in the Culture Industries* (New York, NY: New York University Press).

S. Jones (2007) 'Dickens On Lost: Text, Paratext, Fan-based media', *Wordsworth Circle*, 38(1–2), 71–78.

(3 July 1940) Program for Today at The World's Fair, *The New York Times*.

V. Jouve (1992) *L'effet-personnage dans le roman* (Paris, France: PUF).

L. Klastrup and S. Tosca (2004) 'Transmedial worlds—rethinking cyberworld design', *Proceedings of the International Conference on Cyberworlds*. IEEEE Computer Society, Los Alamitos, CA, http://www.itu.dk/people/klastrup/klastruptosca_transworlds.pdf, date accessed 25 July 2014.

K. C. Lahue (1964) *Continued Next Week: A History of the Moving Picture Serial* (Norman, OK: University of Oklahoma Press).

M. Larrondo (2013) 'El discursopolíticokirchneristahacia la juventud en contextos de actos de militancia', *Astrolabio* 11, 334–363, date accessed 25 April 2014.

D. Lavery (2009) 'Lost and Long-term Television Narrative' in P. Harrigan and N. Wardrip-Fruin (eds) *Third Person. Authoring and Exploring Vast Narratives* (Cambridge, MA: The MIT Press), 313–322.

G. Lippi (1989) 'Introduzione' in R. Howard, *L'era di Conan*, 3–10 (Milano, Italy: Mondadori).

DOI: 10.1057/9781137434371.0010

R. Lobato, J. Thomas and D. Hunter (2011) 'Histories of User-generated Content: Between Formal and Informal Media Economies', *International Journal of Communication*, 5, 899–914, http://ijoc.org/index.php/ijoc/article/view/981, date accessed 25 July 2014.

G. Long (2007) *Transmedia storytelling. Business, aesthetics and production at the Jim Henson Company.* Master's dissertation, Comparative Media Studies, MIT, Cambridge (MA), MIT, http://cms.mit.edu/research/theses/GeoffreyLong2007.pdf, date accessed 25July 2014.

P. Lopes (2009) *Demanding Respect: The Evolution of the American Comic Book* (Philadelphia, PA: Temple University Press).

G. Lord (1976) *The Last Celt: A Bio-Bibliography of Robert Ervin Howard* (West Kingston, RI: D.M. Grant).

P. Louinet (2003) 'Hyborian Genesis: Part 1' in R. Howard, *The Coming of Conan the Cimmerian* (New York, NY: Del Rey), 429–452.

P. Marek (1997–1998) 'Some Comments on Chronologies in Regards to the Conan Series', *REHupa*, 148 and 149.

G. Marrone (2003) *Montalbano. Affermazioni e trasformazioni di un eroe mediatico* (Roma. Italy: Rai-Eri).

B. Martin and F. Ringham (2000) *Dictionary of Semiotics* (London and New York: Cassel).

G. Meikle and S. Young (2012) *Media Convergence: Networked Digital Media in Everyday Life* (London, UK: Palgrave Macmillan).

P. S. Miller and J. D. Clarke (1938) 'A Probable Outline of Conan's Career', *The Hyborian Age*, http://www.barbariankeep.com/career.html, date accessed 21 March 2014.

J. Mittel (2006) 'Narrative Complexity in Contemporary American Television', *The Velvet Light Trap*, 58, https://seguecommunity.middlebury.edu/view/html/site/jmittell/node/4230077, date accessed 21 July 2014.

A. S. Montero (2012) *¡Y al final un día volvimos! Los usos de la memoria en el discurso kirchnerista (2003-2007)* (Buenos Aires, Argentina: Prometeo).

A. S. Montero and L. Vincent (2013) 'Del "peronismo impuro" al "kirchnerismo impuro": la construcción de una nueva identidad política durante la Presidencia de Néstor Kirchner en Argentina (2003–2007)', *RevistaPOSTdata*, 29 April, http://www.revistapostdata.com.ar (home page), date accessed 25 April 2014.

DOI: 10.1057/9781137434371.0010

J. C. Morhain (s/d). *El viajero de la eternidad (o el Eternauta en el teatro)*,http://www.portalcomic.com/, (home page), date accessed 25 April 2014.

S. Moskowitz (1989) *The Immortal Storm: A History of Science Fiction Fandom* (New York, NY: Hyperion Books).

(22 October 1940) The Laugh's on You and Me. *The Washington Post.*

R. Odin (2000) *De la fiction* (Bruxelles, Belgium: De Boeck & Larcier).

R. Pearson (ed.) (2009) *Reading Lost: Perspectives on a Hit Television Show* (London, UK: I.B. Tauris).

N. Perryman (2008) 'Doctor Who and the convergence of media. A case study in transmedia storytelling', *Convergence: The International Journal of Research into New Media Technologies*, 14(1), 21–39.

F. Pohl (1978) *The Way the Future Was: A Memoir* (New York, NY: Del Rey Books).

R. Piglia (2014) 'De la palabra a los acontecimientos', *Página 12*, 5 May, http://www.pagina12.com.ar (home page), date accessed 25 April 2014.

J. Prida (2013) 'Introduction' in J. Prida (ed.) *Conan Meets the Academy*, 5–12 (Jefferson, NC: McFarland & Company).

S. Proietti (2007) 'Ombrerosse: rileggendo Robert E. Howard', *Delos,* 100,http://www.fantascienza.com (home page), date accessed 14 April 2014.

V. Propp (1958) *Morphology of the Folktale* (The Hague, The Netherlands: Mouton).

S. Redmond (2004) *Liquid Metal: The Science Fiction Film Reader* (London, UK: Wallflower Press).

R. T. Reed (1997) 'The Pulps: Their Weaknesses Were Their Strengths' in R. Lesser (ed.) *Pulp Art: Original Cover Paintings for the Great American Pulp Magazines* (New York, NY: Gramercy Books), 44–51.

F. Reggiani (2011) Las aventuras de Nestornauta, 25 February, http://hablandodelasunto.com.ar (home page), date accessed 25 April 2014.

D. Rippke (2003) 'The Dark Storm Conan Chronology. A Post-Modern look at Conan's life according to the writings of Robert E. Howard', *REHupa*, 180, 181, 182, 183. Revised version: http://www.rehupa.com/rippke_chronology.htm, date accessed 21 March 2014.

R. Ronen (1994) *Possible Worlds in Literary Theory* (Cambridge, MA: Cambridge University Press).

E. Rosh (1978) 'Principles of categorization' in E. Rosh & B. Lloyd (Eds.), *Cognition and categorization*, 27–48 (Hillsdale, NJ: Lawrence Erlbaum).

DOI: 10.1057/9781137434371.0010

A. Russo (2002) 'The Dark(ened) Figure on the Airwaves: Race, Nation, and The Green Hornet' in M. Hilmes and J. Loviglio (eds) *Radio Reader: Essays in the Cultural History of Radio* (New York, NY: Routledge), 257–276.

M.-L. Ryan (2004) *Narrative across Media: The Languages of Storytelling* (Lincoln, NE: University of Nebraska Press).

M.-L. Ryan (2005) 'On the Theoretical Foundations of Transmedial Narratology' in J. C. Meister (ed.) *Narrative Beyond Literary Criticism*, 1–23 (Berlin, Germany: De Gruyter).

M.-L. Ryan (2013) 'Transmedial Storytelling and Transfictionality', *Poetics Today*, 34(3), 362–388.

P. M. Sammon (2007) *Conan the Phenomenon: The Legacy of Robert E. Howard's Fantasy Icon* (Milwaukee, WI: Dark Horse Books).

A. Santo (2010) '*Batman* versus *The Green Hornet*: The Merchandisable TV Text and the Paradox of Licensing in the Classical Network Era', *Cinema Journal*, 49(2, Fall).

J. Sasturain (1982) 'El Eternauta no tiene quien le escriba', *Medios y Comunicación*, 17. Included in J. Sasturain (1995) *El Domicilio de la Aventura* (Buenos Aires, Argentina: Colihue).

J. Sasturain (1995) *El Domicilio de la Aventura* (Buenos Aires, Argentina: Colihue).

J. Sasturain (2012) *Oesterheld, el aventurador*, http://www.educ.ar (home page), date accessed 25 April 2014.

D. Saunders (2012) 'The Pulps and the Comics', *Major Malcolm Wheeler-Nicholson*, 22 June, http://malcolmwheelernicholson.com/2012/06/22/the-pulps-and-the-comics/ (home page), date accessed 21 September 2012.

C. A. Scolari (1998) *Historietas para Sobrevivientes. Cómic y cultura de masas en los años 1980* (Buenos Aires, Argentina: Colihue).

C. A. Scolari (2009a) 'Transmedia Storytelling: Implicit Consumers, Narrative Worlds, and Branding in Contemporary Media Production', *International Journal of Communication* 3, 586–606, http://ijoc.org (home page), date accessed 20 November 2013.

C. A. Scolari (2009b) 'The Grammar of Hypertelevision. An Identikit of the Convergence Age Television (Or How Television is Simulating New Interactive Media)', *Journal of Visual Literacy* 28(1), 28–49.

C. A. Scolari (2012) 'The Triplets and the Incredible Shrinking Narrative: Playing in the Borderland between Transmedia

DOI: 10.1057/9781137434371.0010

Storytelling and Adaptation' in I. Ibrus and C. A. Scolari (eds) *Crossmedia Innovations: Texts, Markets, Institutions*, 45–60 (Frankfurt, Germany: Peter Lang).

C. A. Scolari (2013a) *Narrativas Transmedia. Cuando todos los medios cuentan* (Barcelona, Spain: Deusto).

C. A. Scolari (2013b) 'Lostology: Transmedia Storytelling and Expansion/Compression Strategies', *Semiotica* 195, 45–68. doi: 10.1515/sem-2013-0038.

C. A. Scolari (2014) 'Don Quixote of La Mancha: Transmedia Storytelling in the Grey Zone', *International Journal of Communication*, 8, 2382-2405, http://ijoc.org/index.php/ijoc/article/view/2576, date accessed 15 September 2014, doi 1932 -8036/20140005.

J. Scott (2009) 'The Character-Orientated Franchise: Promotion and Exploitation of Pre-Sold Characters in American Film, 1913–1950', *Scope: An Online Journal of Film and Television Studies*, 26, http://www.nottingham.ac.uk/scope/february-issue-26.aspx, date accessed 6 April 2014.

J. Shanks (2013) 'Hyborian Age Archaeology: Unearthing Historical and Anthropological Foundations' in J. Prida (ed.) *Conan Meets the Academy*, 13–34 (Jefferson, NC: McFarland & Company).

B. Singer (1990) Female Power in the Serial-Queen Melodrama, *Camera Obscura,* 22, 90–129.

A. Smith (2009) *Transmedia storytelling in television 2.0.* Unpublished master's thesis. Middlebury College, Middlebury, VT, http://blogs.middlebury.edu/mediacp/, date accessed 18 April 2014.

A. Smith (2012) 'Media contexts of narrative design: Dimensions of specificity within storytelling industries'. Unpublished thesis, University of Nottingham, UK.

E. A. Smith (2000) *Hard-Boiled: Working-Class Readers and Pulp Magazines* (Philadelphia, PA: Temple University Press).

G. Steirer (2011) Narrative Worlds: A Provisional Definition, *Cultural Production,* http://culturalproductionblog.com (home page), date accessed 2 December 2011.

M. Tetro (2004) *Conan il barbaro. L'epica di John Milius* (Alessandria, Italy: Falsopiano).

J. R. R. Tolkien (1964) 'On Fairy Stories', in *Tree and Leaf* (London, UK: Allen & Unwin), 3–83.

D. Tomasi (1988) *Cinema e racconto. Il personaggio* (Torino, Italy: Loescher).

DOI: 10.1057/9781137434371.0010

S. Tompkins (2006) 'Introduction', in R. Howard, *Kull. Exile of Atlantis* (New York, NY: Del Rey Books), xix–xxix.

W. Uricchio and R. Pearson (1991) 'I'm Not Fooled by That Cheap Disguise' in W. Uricchio and R. Pearson (eds) *The Many Lives of the Batman: Critical Approaches to a Superhero and His Media* (New York, NY: Routledge), 182–213.

E. Verón and S. Sigal (1986) *Perón o Muerte. Los fundamentos discursivos del fenómeno peronista* (Buenos Aires, Argentina: Legasa).

E. Waterman (2014) *The Chronology Controversy*, http://www.barbariankeep.com/chronx.html, date accessed 22 March 2014.

M. J. P. Wolf (2012) *Building Imaginary Worlds: The Theory and History of Subcreation* (New York, NY: Routledge).

W. H. Jr. Young (1969) 'The Serious Funnies: Adventure Comics During the Depression 1929–1938', *Journal of Popular Culture* 3(3, Winter).

Fictional works

Action Comics #1 (June 1938), National Allied Publications [DC Comics].

Action Comics #6 (November 1938), National Allied Publications [DC Comics].

Age of Conan: Hyborian Adventures. MMORPG.Funcom – Eidos Interactive, 2008.

G. Arnold (10 December 1978) Hollywood's Super Holiday. *The Washington Post*.

Atom Man vs. Superman. Film, directed by Spencer Gordon Bennet. USA, Columbia Pictures, 1950.

Batman. Film, directed by Lambert Hillyer. USA, Columbia Pictures, 1943.

Buck Rogers (7 January 1929). National Newspaper Service.

'*Buck Rogers*' Mutual Broadcasting System. 1 July 1932.

E. R. Burroughs (1912) Tarzan of the Apes. *The All-Story*. Frank A. Munsey Company.

E. R. Burroughs (1912) Under the Moons of Mars. *The All-Story*. Frank A. Munsey Company.

E. R. Burroughs (1913) The Return of Tarzan. *New Story Magazine*. LaSalle Publishing Co.

E. R. Burroughs (1914) At the Earth's Core. *The All-Story*. Frank A. Munsey Company.

E. R. Burroughs (1916) Tarzan and the Jewels of Opar. *The All-Story*. Frank A. Munsey Company.

DOI: 10.1057/9781137434371.0010

E. R. Burroughs (1918) The Land That Time Forgot. *Blue Book Magazine.* Story-Press Corporation.

Close Encounters of the Third Kind. Film, directed by Steven Spielberg. USA, EMI Films, 1977.

Conan, #1–50 (2004–2008). Dark Horse Comics.

Conan and the Young Warriors. Animated TV series. USA, CBS, 1994.

Conan the Adventurer. Animated TV series. USA, Fox, 1992–1993.

Conan the Adventurer. Live action TV series. USA, syndicated, 1997–1998.

Conan the Avenger, #1-ongoing (2014–). Dark Horse Comics.

Conan the Barbarian #1–275 (1970–1993). Marvel Comics Group.

Conan the Barbarian. Newspaper comic strip. (4 September 1978 – 12 April 1981).

Conan the Barbarian. Film, directed by John Milius. USA, Twentieth Century Fox, 1982.

Conan the Barbarian. Film, directed by Jason Momoa. USA, Paradox Entertainment, 2011

Conan the Barbarian, #1–25 (2012–2014). Dark Horse Comics.

Conan the Cimmerian, #1–26 (2008–2010). Dark Horse Comics.

Conan the Destroyer. Film, directed by Richard Fleischer. USA, Universal Pictures, 1984.

Conan: Road of Kings, #1–12 (2010–2012). Dark Horse Comics.

L. S. De Camp (1979) *Conan the Liberator* (New York: Bantam)

L. S. De Camp and L. Carter (1977) *Conan of Aquilonia* (New York: Ace Books)

L. S. De Camp and L. Carter (1982) *Conan the Barbarian* (New York: Bantam)

L. S. De Camp, L. Carter and B. Nyberg (1978) *Conan the Swordsman* (New York: Bantam)

Detective Comics #27 (May 1939), National Allied Publications [DC Comics].

Doctor Who. BBC. 1963–Present.

Hamilton, E. (1942) *Planets in Peril*, Popular Library.

Heroes. NBC. 2006–2010.

R. E. Howard (1929) The Shadow Kingdom. *Weird Tales.* Popular Fiction Publishing.

R. E. Howard (1932) The Phoenix on the Sword. *Weird Tales.* Popular Fiction Publishing.

R. E. Howard (1933) The Slithering Shadows. *Weird Tales.* Popular Fiction Publishing.

DOI: 10.1057/9781137434371.0010

R. E. Howard (1934) Gods of the North. *The Fantasy Fan.* Charles D. Hornig.

R. E. Howard (1934) The Queen of the Black Coast. *Weird Tales.* Popular Fiction Publishing.

R. E. Howard (1936) The Hour of the Dragon. *Weird Tales.* Popular Fiction Publishing.

R. E. Howard (1938) *The Hyborian Age* (Los Angeles - New York: LANY Cooperative Publications).

R. E. Howard [extensively rewritten by L.S. De Camp] (1953), 'The Treasure of Tranicos', in *King Conan* (New York: Gnome Press).

R. E. Howard [extensively rewritten by L.S. De Camp] (1955), *Tales of Conan* (New York: Gnome Press).

R. E. Howard (1967) By This Axe I Rule, in R. Howard and L. Carter, *King Kull* (New York: Lancer).

R. E. Howard (1976) 'The Frost Giant's Daughter', in *Rogues in the House* (Hampton Falls: Donald M. Grant).

R. E. Howard (2003) *The Conan Chronicles. Volume 1: The People of the Black Circle* (London: Gollancz, 2003).

R. E. Howard (2003) *The Conan Chronicles. Volume 2: The Hour of the Dragon* (London: Gollancz, 2003).

King Conan, #1-ongoing (2011–). Dark Horse Comics.

King Conan/Conan the King #1–55 (1974–1995). Marvel Comics Group.

I. Kordey (2000) *Batman/Tarzan: Claws of the Cat-Woman.* London, Titan Books.

C. S. Lewis (1950–1956) *Chronicles of Narnia* (London: Geoffrey Bles and London: The Bodley Head).

A. Merrit (1924) The Ship of Ishtar. *Argosy All-Story Weekly.* G. P. Putnam's Sons.

New York World's Fair (1940), National Allied Publications [DC Comics].

B. Nyberg and L. S. De Camp (1957) *The Return of Conan* (New York: Gnome Press).

H. G. Oesterheld and F. Solano López (1975) *El Eternauta* (Buenos Aires: Record). Compilation of the original comics published in *Hora Cero Semanal* (1957–1959).

H. G. Oesterheld (1995) *El Eternauta y otroscuentos de cienciaficción* (Buenos Aires: Colihue).

A. J. Offutt (1978) *Conan and the Sorcerer* (New York: Ace Books).

A. J. Offutt (1981) *Conan the Mercenary* (New York: Ace Books).

N. Page (1939) Flame Winds. *Unknown.* Street & Smith Publications.

DOI: 10.1057/9781137434371.0010

Savage Tales #1–5 (1971–1975). Marvel Comics Group.

Simonson, W. (1997) *Tarzan vs. Predator: At Earth's Core*. London, Dark Horse.

Star Wars. Film, directed by George Lucas. USA, Lucas film, 1977.

Superman (January 1939), The McClure Newspaper Syndicate.

Superman #158 (January 1963), National Allied Publications [DC Comics].

Superman. Film, directed by Spencer Gordon Bennet.USA, Columbia Pictures, 1948.

'*The Adventures of Superman*' Mutual Broadcasting System. 12 February 1940.

'*The Green Hornet*' Mutual Broadcasting System. 31 January 1936.

'*The Lone Ranger*' Mutual Broadcasting System. 30 January 1933.

The Matrix. Film, directed by Larry and Andy Wachowski.USA, Warner Bros., 1999.

The Phantom. Film, directed by B. Reeves Eason.USA, Columbia Pictures, 1943.

The Savage Sword of Conan the Barbarian #1–235 (1974–1995). Marvel Comics Group.

'*The Shadow*' Mutual Broadcasting System. 26 September 1937.

The Shadow. Film, directed by James W. Horne.USA, Columbia Pictures, 1940.

The Shadow (17 June 1931). The Ledger Syndicate.

2001: A Space Odyssey. Film, directed by Stanley Kubrick. USA, MGM, 1968.

J. R. R. Tolkien (1954–1955) *The Lord of the Rings* (London: Allen & Unwin).

J. Verne (1865) *From the Earth to the Moon* (Paris: Pierre-Jules Hetzel).

What Happened to Mary? Film, directed by Charles Brabin. USA, Thomas A. Edison, Inc., 1912.

Wonder Woman #70 (November 1954), National Allied Publications [DC Comics].

DOI: 10.1057/9781137434371.0010

Index

9781137301321oo11

DOI: 10.1057/9781137301321.0011

DOI: 10.1057/9781137301321.0011

DOI: 10.1057/9781137301321.0011

DOI: 10.1057/9781137301321.0011

Lightning Source UK Ltd.
Milton Keynes UK
UKOW04n1702071215

264268UK00003B/16/P